D0929088

AL CHET

עַל חֵטְא

AL CHET

SINS IN THE MARKETPLACE

MEIR TAMARI

JASON ARONSON INC.
Northvale, New Jersey
London

The author gratefully acknowledges permission to quote from Isaac Levy, trans., *The Hirsch Chumash*. Copyright © 1962 The Judaica Press. Used by permission of The Judaica Press, Brooklyn, NY.

This book was set in 11 pt. Garamond by Alpha Graphics of Pittsfield, New Hampshire.

10 9 8 7 6 5 4 3 2 1

Library of Congress Cataloging-in-Publication Data

Tamari, Meir.
Al chet : sins in the marketplace / Meir Tamari.
p. cm.
Includes bibliographical references and index.
ISBN 1-56821-906-7 (alk. paper)
1. Repentance—Judaism. 2. Economics—Religious aspects—Judaism.
I. Title.
BM645.R45T36 1996
296.3'85—dc20 95-52779
CIP

Manufactured in the United States of America. Jason Aronson Inc. offers books and cassettes. For information and catalog write to Jason Aronson Inc., 230 Livingston Street, Northvale, New Jersey 07647.

Righteousness is the positive action
for those things that Justice comes to rectify.

Samson Raphael Hirsch
on Deuteronomy 6:24

Contents

Preface

This book is the fourth I have written concerning business, economics, and Jewish ethical thought and practice. Yet I feel that perhaps it is really the beginning of the cycle, as in this book I have primarily let the sources speak for themselves.

It is a fitting time to thank the many friends and colleagues who, for the past twenty years, have provided insights, guidance, and encouragement in the various areas discussed in these books: Businessmen like Mr. Fred Worms, Mr. Clive Marks, Mr. David Schreiber, Mr. Peter Kalms, all of London; the late Mr. Ludwig Jesselson of New York; and academics like Professor Eli Schwartz of Lehigh University, Professor Jonas Prager of New York University, Professor Leo Levi and Professor Yaacov Zeisel of the Jerusalem College of Technology, and Professor Lawrence Klein of Wharton; Rabbi A. Shulman, Rabbi M. J. Lebel, and Rabbi M. Goldstein of Telz-Stone, and Rabbi Simon Schwab, *z'l*, of Washington Heights, New York. Special mention must be made of Rabbi Simcha Wasserman, *z'l*, of Jerusalem, who for many years consistently encouraged me and recognized the great importance of work in this field of Jewish business ethics.

I would like to thank Mr. David Jackson, who helped research some of the material used in this book, and Mrs. Zissie Gitel, who generously gave of her time to type much of the manuscript.

Introduction

Viduy, "confession," is the centerpiece of the prayers on Yom Kippur and the fitting culmination of the Days of Awe that start on Rosh Hashanah and end on the Day of Atonement. The scenes of white-robed figures in crowded synagogues, beating their breasts in sorrow form major themes of the pictorial representation of this day. Recited silently and repeated in public prayer, this *Al Chet*, confession of the sins we have committed individually and collectively, is after all the prerequisite for any atonement and forgiveness. Unfortunately sometimes the significance of the confession somehow gets lost. This may be due to familiarity and repetitiveness which makes the recitation mechanical. Sometimes, the opposite is true, and it is the strangeness of the language or ignorance that makes it mere ritual. Whatever the cause, a major spiritual dimension may be lost to us. This book is offered as a possible alternative. It is hoped that study before Yom Kippur and its use during the service may help to create a suitable environment for the modern man and woman to true confession and the promised atonement.

One of the major themes of *viduy* is social immorality and unethical behavior. More of the verses of the *Al Chet* refer to this theme than to any other spiritual or religious shortcoming. This is natural not only because of Judaism's this-worldly concern but also because while Yom Kippur itself brings atonement for ritual or God-oriented shortcomings, it does not atone for sins between people. These require a specific confession before atonement can be achieved. Nowhere are these sins more common and pervasive than in the marketplace, in the pursuit of wealth, and in our patterns of consumption. Our activities as entrepreneurs, creditors, or debtors, employers or employees, producers or consumers, and as citizens or officials of the state, form the theme of the *Al Chet* described in this book.

Throughout the book, I have primarily presented textual material drawn from the Bible, the *Mishnah* and Talmud, the homiletic literature, and moralistic texts, as well as sayings and stories of our rabbis in different generations and countries. My own observations have been kept to a minimum so as to allow the readers to experience for themselves the spiritual power and the relevance of Torah sources in these aspects of our present-day behavior.

The first three chapters present the idea of *teshuvah*, "repentance," in general and its application to business ethics in the home, in the marketplace, and in society. They also show the actions required in Judaism for this repentance to be worthy of divine forgiveness.

The list of sins relevant to our wealth is a long one, but only thirteen of them are discussed in full detail. This was done to minimize repetition and also to keep the text concise. In every case source material is provided to show the relevance of age-old texts to even the most modern and sophisticated economies. Sometimes the application is obvious as in the chapters dealing with *kapat shochad*—by bribery; *khachas u'khazav*—fraud and falsehood; *masah umatan*—business and commerce; *neshekh umarbit*—usury and interest. The others however are perhaps even more important because our sources show them to be hidden agendas for business and economic immorality. So the chapters on *yodim velo yodim*—wittingly and unwittingly—are the rationalization of deceitful acts that permit the development of "gray areas" in morality; *azut metzach*—brazen arrogance—enables us to browbeat competitors, employees, and debtors, to default on debts and obligations; *daat umirmah*—deceitfully—is the deceiving and misleading through advertising, withholding relevant financial or other relevant data, and even by creating false expectations or impressions; *imutz halev*—callousness—whereby we ignore the needs of the distressed and disadvantaged, harass those in our employment and shame staff or peers; *chozek yod*—violence—this is the nonphysical violence done when due wages are withheld, by denying loans that were received, by abusing trust funds or clients' money and by in any way coercing people to buy or sell something against their original inclination; *honaat re'ah*—oppression of a fellow person—this is overcharging, excessive profiteering, taking advantage of another person's ignorance of market conditions or of his financial distress.

Other chapters present the spiritual dimensions of business and commercial activity, which provide the only real bulwark against immorality since without a spiritual dimension and education, no code or legal framework can be effective. *B'giluy uvaseter*—almost all economic crime occurs when hidden from public scrutiny. Insider trading, nondisclosure of material information, using false weights or measures, deceptive packaging, copying of computer programs or other protected material are all examples of secret crimes so there is an *al chet* for these actions done in public and in secret, since there is nothing hidden from God. *Bechillul hashem*—desecrating God's Name—is one of the most serious crimes envisaged in Judaism. The Talmud cites economic misbehavior as one of the most prevalent actions that bring Jews and the Jewish God into disgrace. Fraudulent bankruptcy, white collar crime, tax evasion, and money laundering are unfortunately common examples. The subsequent defamation of God's name depends on the degree of Jewish identity, learning, or communal status of the perpetrator.

B'yetzer hara—by our ability to do evil—in the economic field is probably the most powerful of all the human impulses. It weakens neither with age nor affluence and often overpowers considerations of family or nation. *Bemaachal u'v'mishteh*—in eating and drinking—extends far beyond simple gluttony. The blurring of distinctions between needs and wants and the insistent search for a constantly rising standard of living, spurred by our consumer oriented society and conspicuous consumption, are the primary sources of dishonesty.

In chapter 17 Judaism's antidote to the long list of *Al Chet* is presented. Education and role models conceived in the obligation "to do that which is good and righteous" lead to actions beyond the letter of the law. Voluntary renunciation of legitimate legal rights is shown to be the imprint of Jewish economic righteousness while "what's mine is yours and yours is yours" is our concept of saintliness. The economics of "enough" is substituted for "more is better than less," and so the economic *yetzer hara* may be educated and sanctified bringing atonement for all of the *Al Chet*.

Psalm 15 is the epilogue to this book. The psalm reiterates the theme flowing through our repentance for the sins of the marketplace. Here David presents eleven cardinal principles of Jewish observance, all of which concern the earning and spending of money.

1

TESHUVAH

INTRODUCTION

"If a person transgressed any of the *mitzvot*, irrespective of whether they are positive or negative ones, and decides to repent, they are obligated to make a confession. This applies whether the acts were deliberate or accidental. Such a verbal confession is a positive *mitzvah* even as it is written (Numbers 5:6–7), 'and every man or woman . . . shall confess the sins they have committed'" (Rambam, *Hilkhot Teshuvah*, chap. 1, *halakhah* 1).

Although it is important and acceptable to repent and to confess throughout the year, the ten days from Rosh Hashanah culminating in Yom Kippur are especially propitious and conducive. This is the period of judgment and forgiveness that must be preceded by acknowledgment of our sins and the undertaking not to repeat them.

Contrary to what one may think, this process of repentance and confession is not a morbid involvement with the dark recesses of human thought and action. Rather "It is a great mercy which the Almighty has given to His creatures. He has thereby prepared for them a pathway out of the guilt-filled pit and an escape out of the conscience-racked trap of their offenses. [It is this gift of repentance that enables people] to save themselves from destruction. . . . Even if they have offended, rebelled and corrupted, He has not closed before them the gates of repentance" (Rabbi Jonah of Gerondi, Italy, *Shaarei Teshuvah*, First Gate, sec. 1).

"The *Midrash* teaches us that the gates of prayer are like a well but the gates of *teshuvah* are like the waters of the ocean. This is so because prayer requires an '*eit ratzon*,' a propitious period, which sometimes exists and sometimes does not. So acceptance of prayer is not a constant. *Teshuvah*, however, is like the ocean, which is never locked nor closed. So the gates of repentance are always open" (Shem MiShmuel, Admor of Sochochow, Poland, 20th century, *Moadim*).

The Divine kindness manifest in the possibility of *teshuvah* reechoes in the penitential prayers and throughout the Days of Judgment and Atonement. We address our prayers not only to the King-Judge but also to our Father. We come before Him as children to a Father secure in His love and His kindness, which will help us overcome our shortcomings and cleanse us of past sins. *Teshuvah* is an admission of man's weaknesses yet at the same time a reaffirmation of the divine elements in him that allow him to respond to the Father's love.

Repentance, rejection of misdeeds, and confession are therefore optimistic avenues for us to cleanse ourselves spiritually and thereafter to achieve greater morality and righteousness. However, this Divine kindness must not be construed as a charm that requires simple lip service or momentary remorse. As in all other aspects of life, here too, Judaism presents definite guidelines for action and for assuming responsibility.

The following guidelines, codified by Maimonides, are repeated in all of our sources: legal decisions, homiletical literature, and biblical commentary.

The Principles of Repentance

"What is proper repentance? [This is achieved when] the opportunity occurs for an immoral act which one has committed in the past, and it is possible to perform it [once again; however one] refrains from doing this act out of *Teshuvah* but not out of fear [of punishment] nor out of lack of ability or capacity.

"This is [the application of] repentance [since] the sinner has ceased to sin, removed it from his very thoughts and has decided not to repeat it. . . . In addition it is necessary to feel and express sorrow about the past deeds [without such regret, one would not really repent]. [Prior to repentance] it is necessary to confess aloud saying 'O God, I have sinned [accidentally] I have erred [deliberately], and have done wrong [in order to anger or as an act of rebellion or with malice.' This verbal confession progresses from the lesser to the greater immorality], and I have done such and such an act or acts [it is impossible to repent without recognizing that one has performed specific immoral or forbidden acts].

"[However] one who confesses without a definite decision to change [and to avoid wrongdoing] is like one who immerses himself in a ritual bath [in order to purify himself] even while holding on to the corpse [which made him impure in the first place] since the immersion is of no avail until he discards the *sheretz* [the corpse]. It is extremely meritorious for the penitent to confess in public and to announce his crimes to others. [He should] reveal his sins 'between man and man' to others [so that they may intercede for him to those whom he has wronged. (Rashi, *Yoma* 36b)] and he says to them 'Behold I have sinned against so and so and done such and such an action but today I repent and am filled with remorse' [often one lacks the courage to admit errors and then it becomes necessary to rationalize or to hide the acts. So] those arrogant people who do not confess their sins publicly but cover them, they do not repent in truth. [The obligation of public particularization of sins refers] only to sins between man and man; regarding those sins against Heaven [such] public confession is a sign of arrogance" (*Mishneh Torah*, *Hilkhot Teshuvah*, chap. 2, *halakhot* 1–5).

"The root of this *mitzvah* [of confession] is that verbal particularization of the sins and errors reveals the acceptance by the penitent of the truth that the all-seeing God knows and sees even the most secret of the actions of mankind" (*Sefer HaChinukh, mitzvah* 463).

This awareness of the personal Deity, before whom all things are clearly known and evident, and the necessity to reform and correct one's misdeeds and immorality in order to avoid His inevitable punishment are a sine qua non for any real *teshuvah*. This awareness militates against secret crimes, against plotting, conniving, and oppression. It limits the possibilities for white-collar crime, victimless crime, and fraud.

Forgiveness

"It is customary in the world that one who has a court case, dresses in mourning . . . allows his beard to grow [a sign of mourning] . . . as he is fearful of the consequences . . . but Israel dresses [on Rosh Hashanah—day of judgment] in white . . . trims the beard [signs of rejoicing] eats, drinks, and is happy because . . . he knows that God will [in his mercy] perform a miracle [and forgive all the sins]" (*Tur*, *Orach Chaim*, sec. 581).

"This is not just intuitive knowledge but is clearly spelled out in the Torah, 'And on this day [Yom Kippur] I [God] will surely forgive you' (Leviticus 16:30). It is repeated throughout the Bible. 'Let the wicked give up his ways . . . let him turn back to the Lord who will have pity on him, to our God who pardons abundantly' (Isaiah 55:7). And repentance [today in the absence of the Temple and the sacrificial service of Yom Kippur] brings forgiveness for all sins [even though the stages of forgiveness vary according to the severity of the punishment for the sin, as explained below]. Even one who is evil all his days and does *teshuvah* toward the end of his life, we are not allowed to remind him of his evil deeds . . . even as it is written 'the evil deeds will not cause one to fail in the days of his repentance' (Ezekiel 33:12). Repentance brings in its wake forgiveness for everything, and Yom Kippur itself causes forgiveness [for those who repent, yet] there are sins which are immediately and finally forgiven [and other] sins which are only forgiven after time [or other actions]. . . .One who transgresses a positive *mitzvah*, whose punishment is *karet* [Divine severance of the sinner's life and his ties to the Jewish People; for example, deliberate eating of leavened bread on Seder night] when he repents, he is immediately forgiven. *Teshuvah* for transgression of a negative *mitzvah* that does not involve *karet* [for example, wearing *shatnez* (mixture of diverse fibers)] and does not involve the death penalty is held in abeyance until Yom Kippur, which brings forgiveness" (*Mishneh Torah*, *Hilkhot Teshuvah*, chap. 1, *halakhot* 3–4).

Yet the King God who is eternally aware of our actions, before whom there is neither bribery nor forgetfulness and who severely punishes transgressors, is also the Father of Mankind and the source of kindness, mercy, and forgiveness. So the transgressions between man and man introduce a further element into this equation of justice and mercy. They involve not only the individual's transgressions of God's justice but also the suffering, oppression, and exploitation of other individuals, thereby demanding additional forms of *Teshuvah* before forgiveness can be attained.

The first stage in the *Teshuvah* process for these sins is rectifying the damage done by replacing that which was stolen or by appeasing the injured party. It is noteworthy that the classic example for the Jews of such an action as a prelude to atonement is taken from the Book of Jonah and relates to the idolatrous gentile people of Assyria. "Regarding the people of Nineveh it is written, 'and the Lord saw by their actions that they had returned from their evil way'" (Jonah 3:10). In an earlier verse the text tells us that "each person repented of their evil ways and [returned] from the violent theft [lit., *chamas*, "that which is only of trivial value"] which was in their hands. For regarding all those transgressions between man and man, like robbery and *chamas*, it is not possible to be forgiven until one has returned the stolen goods or appeased the oppressed. . . . It is fitting for the penitent to do this [repair the damage, and so on] before he makes confession . . ." (*Shaarei Teshuvah*, First Gate, sec. 46).

Rectifying the damage, returning stolen goods, and compensating for fraud, however, are not sufficient. Such acts simply restore the situation to its previous state and do not express regret. Neither is paying the fines levied by the Torah and enforced by a *bet din* sufficient. These acts must be accompanied by the acknowledgment of the sin, remorse, and undertaking not to repeat the economic crime, just as in all other examples of the *Teshuvah* process. Moreover, monetary crimes are not just spiritual matters but also have practical legal consequences, as seen in the following ruling from the Rambam.

"By Torah law [*mide'oraita*, as distinct from rabbinic rulings] the wicked are disqualified from being witnesses even as it is written, 'You shall not join hands with a wicked man that he become an unrighteous witness' (Exodus 23:1). From the Oral Tradition we learn that this enjoins us from appointing wicked people as witnesses (*Talmud Bavli*, *Sanhedrin* 27a). The wicked ones who take other people's money like thieves and robbers even though they have returned the stolen goods [are under constant suspicion that they will take bribes and so] are debarred from being witnesses. . . . Those who bear false witness [even in monetary matters] and were forced by the courts to pay the damage they intended to cause are considered by the Torah to be invalid witnesses for all matters [both in monetary matters and in capital crimes]. So too, those who lend money at interest and those who borrowed the money [this is because of their lust for money (Rashi on *Sanhedrin* 27a), . . . the violent people who buy land or movables against the will of the owners even though they pay for the goods [their lust for money, which prompts such behavior creates suspicion that they will be prepared to take bribes and give false evidence] are not allowed by rabbinic law to be witnesses (*Sanhedrin* 25b). Also the shepherds both of sheep and cattle since we suspect that they will allow them to graze in the fields and plantations of others. Private operators [who buy the concession from the state] are suspect that they will try to [increase their profits by] exceeding the tax levied by the state so they are debarred from being witnesses; this does not apply to government tax officials. The bird racers who are suspect [of theft] in that they teach their birds to bring home the birds belonging to other people. And also those who deal commercially in the produce of the Sabbatical Year [which becomes ownerless during that period. The Torah commanded that the produce be used only for personal consumption but these people in their lust for financial gain trade in it; this lust prevents them from being trustworthy witnesses (Rashi, *Talmud Bavli Sanhedrin* 24b).] Professional gamblers are not valid witnesses since they do not contribute to the development of the world and therefore we consider them guilty of some form of robbery" (*Mishneh Torah, Hilkhot Eidut*, chap. 10).

Then the Rambam goes on to show what is necessary to enable these people to repent, achieve atonement, and thereby be eligible to bear witness. "Those who are not eligible to serve as witnesses [because of the above sins] even if they paid their fines and the damage, need to repent and to confess publicly that they have changed their ways. The moneylenders need to tear up the notes of indebtedness in their possession [which specify the interest. Afterward they can collect their principal on the basis of their verbal evidence (*Meirat Einayim*, *Shulchan Arukh*, *Choshen Mishpat*, sec. 34, subsec. 73)] and undertake not to lend money at interest in the future.

"The gamblers need to break the cards or other tools of their trade, and the bird racers need to destroy the nets and snares with which they catch the birds. Those who trade in produce of the Sabbatical Year do *Teshuvah* when the next *Shmittah* comes and they refrain from their trade [they are not able to replace the produce but this shows their repentance]" (*Mishneh Torah*, *Hilkhot Eidut*, chap. 12, *halakhot* 4–8).

In many cases, the return of stolen goods, repairing damage, and compensating for fraud or theft are possible. But in other cases where many people were victimized or the victims are unknown, redress is impossible. This almost always happens in stock market fraud, large-scale overcharging, deceptive or false advertising, and pyramid schemes. How then will *teshuvah* be possible? Will the sinner who wishes to repent and change his business methods or his financial operations remain spiritually unatoned?

The *Shulchan Arukh*, discussing the punishment of one who defrauds through false weights and measures, provides an ethical perspective and a form of *Teshuvah* for these and allied business crimes.

"The punishment for [possessing or defrauding with faulty] weights and measures is very serious [Maimonides in *Hilkhot Geneivah*, chap. 7, *halakhah* 12, considers it to be worse than sexual immorality, since the latter is a *mitzvah* between man and God while the former is between man and man] since the culprit, either weighing or measuring falsely cannot achieve true atonement [through repaying the fraud, because of the number and anonymity of the victims. It is true that if he does good deeds and gives charity, this is meritorious but it is not *Teshuvah*]" (*Choshen Mishpat*, sec. 231, subsec. 19; see *Meirat Einayim*).

In the days when the Temple stood in Jerusalem, a man or woman who had sinned but had repented could bring a sin offering, make a confession, and be assured of forgiveness. At a national level, the confessions of the High Priest, the sacrifices, and the scapegoat of Yom Kippur obtained forgiveness for all Israel. At both these levels, however, these acts were insufficient to cleanse the transgressions between man and man.

"And the Lord spoke to Moses, saying, if a soul sins and commits a faithlessness against the Lord and denies a deposit he received from his neighbor or a trust or robbed with violence or has exploited his neighbor [withholds wages of workers, but subsequently] denies any of these things that a man does, sinning thereby [and then swears falsely with the object of avoiding a financial obligation]. Then because he has sinned [and now wishes to recognize his error, and repent, confess, and thereby] incur guilt. Then he shall restore that which he stole with violence, or that which he has obtained through coercion, or the deposit which was entrusted to him, or the lost article which he found [and which he was obligated to return but did not, thereby becoming guilty of theft], or whatsoever act he has denied under oath. He shall return the principal and add to it a fine of 20 percent . . . and he shall bring a guilt sacrifice to the Lord . . . and the priest shall extend atonement to him" (Leviticus 5:21–26).

Rabbi Akiva questioned the use of "faithlessness against the Lord" in the above verses dealing with misdeeds between people. He explained that normally one does business in the presence of witnesses or with documentation. So when one denies a transaction or makes false claims, one is rejecting the witnesses or the documents. In all the above cases, however, only God is a witness between the two parties. By denying the deposit or the trust or the found article, he is rejecting God; thus these are acts of faithlessness against the Lord (*Sifra, Leviticus* 5:21).

This idea that economic crimes and social injustice are transgressions against God makes remedying the damage or restoring the property a prerequisite for any atonement. But simply rectifying the misdeeds without any sincere repentance is insufficient for atonement. Without repentance, nothing spiritual is achieved. The discussion in the Talmud led the codifiers to rule that where the culprit made restitution only on the basis of evidence brought against him in a *bet din* but not of his own cognizance, no fine is levied, and he does not bring any sin offering. As long as he has actually never repented, the Torah does not allow him to take these steps toward atonement (see *Mishneh Torah*, *Hilkhot Geneivah*, chap. 4, *halakhah* 1, for an example).

Furthermore, in all cases where there has been no penance for the injustice, fraud, or coercion, the sacrifices prescribed for atonement are of no avail. "And so all those obligated to bring sin offerings or guilt offerings for their deliberate or accidental sins [for theft or for false evidence] are not forgiven, despite their sacrifices, until they repent and verbally confess. So also all those liable to the death penalty or to corporal punishment neither their death nor their lashings bring forgiveness unless they confess and repent. One who causes injury to his fellow, or causes him financial loss or material damage, even though he makes restitution, cannot be forgiven unless he does *teshuvah*" (*Mishneh Torah*, *Hilkhot Teshuvah*, chap. 1, *halakhah* 1).

All the prophets make it clear that the divinely ordained sacrifices require spiritual intent and appropriate behavior. The Temple service on its own and the mandatory sacrifices cannot bring atonement at the national level, without attention to sins between man and man through restitution, confession, and repentance.

After decrying the multitude of sacrifices, burnt offerings, incense, and libations, Isaiah tells Israel that even though these are obligatory for them, nevertheless the Lord does not hear because "your hands are full of blood . . . put away the evil of your doings . . . cease to do evil. Learn to do well; seek judgment, relieve the oppressed, judge [justify or assist] the orphan, and plead for the widow" (Isaiah 1:15–17).

Then come the words of Jeremiah: "Trust ye not in lying words saying 'the Temple of the Lord, the Temple of the Lord, the Temple of the Lord are these.' Only if you will sincerely amend your ways and your actions; if you promote justice between man and his neighbor; if you oppress not the stranger, the orphan, and the widow and shed not innocent blood in this place, neither walk after other gods to bring evil on yourselves. Then I will surely dwell in your midst [in this House] in the Land I have given to your fathers for eternity" (Jeremiah 7:4–7).

This message of the relationships between the positive effect of sacrificial worship and economic morality is repeated throughout the prophets, exemplified by the following words of Amos: "Though you offer me burnt offerings and your meat offerings, I will not accept them nor will I regard the peace offering of your fat beasts. Take away from me the noise of songs of prayer for I will not hear the melody of your harps [accompanying the Temple service]. Rather let judgment run down as waters and righteousness as a mighty stream" (Amos 5:22–24).

The *Midrash* reiterates this relationship between morality and the acceptability of Temple service and the sacrifices when it comments on the detailed plans of the Third Temple set out in chapter 43 of Ezekiel. "Isaiah (61:8) said, 'Because I am God who loves Justice and hates theft in the daily offering'. . . the Holy One, Blessed Be He, says, 'One should not say one will rob and oppress and then bring an offering and thereby one will be forgiven. For I, God, hate the dishonesty even in the offerings which they do regarding their theft. If a man wants that his offerings should be accepted, he should return the illegal and immoral wealth earned to its owners and then his offering will be accepted'" (*Midrash Tanchuma*, *Tzav* 14).

2

In the Marketplace, in the Workplace, and in the Home

Introduction

"If God will be with me and protect me on this path that I am treading and will give me bread to eat and clothes to wear . . ." (Genesis 28:20). In his oath, the Patriarch Jacob prayed first for protection and only then for food and clothing, expressing the spiritual and religious guidance needed in the search for wealth and material goods. Without such guidance, injustice, dishonesty, fraud, and oppression easily become acceptable ways of earning a living and satisfying economic needs and want. Ever since Adam and Eve were expelled from the Garden of Eden, earning one's daily bread, providing an acceptable standard of living, and preserving one's wealth have become as difficult as the miracle needed to split the Red Sea for the Israelites leaving Egypt.

"Without God's protection and the framework provided by Torah, people will give up their very beings to achieve material goals. Then in the pursuit of livelihood and social status, God is denied, morality is abandoned, a neighbor's property, life, or honor is unprotected, and even respect for marriage and sexual purity is lost" (Samson Raphael Hirsch on Genesis, 6:11).

This is a reflection of the power of the "*yetzer hara*," the evil inclination for money and wealth. Indeed this inclination, both in its power for good and for evil, is more powerful than any other of the lusts or desires that people have. It is a lust that is never satisfied no matter how much it is fed, a desire that is never completely fulfilled. Physical weakness and old age do not blunt this lust as they do other human desires. Rare is the person who believes that he has enough money or has acquired sufficient wealth. The rabbis tell us that "one has a hundred coins yet desires two hundred" (*Midrash, Kohelet Rabbah* 1:34).

Torah education, religious status, and even spiritual achievement may blunt, control, or minimize this *yetzer hara*, but they do not totally eradicate it. All people, irrespective of their position, may fall foul of the pernicious effects that wealth and the striving for it so often produce. It is noteworthy that even Moses, Samuel, and Samson all found it necessary to declare that they had not taken the property of others nor exploited their sanctified positions in order to benefit materially.

It seems that because of the power of economic lust and its pervasiveness, the Torah surrounded it with more *mitzvot* (over 100) than it did, for example, for kosher food (for which there are only 28 *mitzvot*). The Chafetz Chaim found eleven *mitzvot* related to talebearing, slander, and *lashon hara*. Obviously the disparity in no way reduces the importance or severity of these or other aspects of Judaism; it simply shows that many guardians and much spiritual protection in the form of *mitzvot* are essential if this most powerful *yetzer* is to be elevated and made holy.

Needs and Wants

Because of the insatiable nature of economic drive, the time, effort, and ability invested in satisfying wants and needs easily become a treadmill from which it is almost impossible to escape. The obsessiveness fueling the treadmill makes it often difficult to distinguish between permitted and forbidden acts, to allocate time for obligatory Torah learning, and to save a place for the demands of wife and family.

Because of the great increase in economic production and the efficiency of modern distribution, basic economic needs can now be satisfied by legal and moral efforts more easily than at any other period in human history. Unfortunately, while needs are relatively few, wants are unlimited. The consumer society geared to "more is always better than less," to age-old human greed, and to coveting what others have constantly turns all wants into needs. The inability to echo our Father Jacob's "I have everything" means that contemporary patterns of spending, the ever-spiraling standards of living, and the social status expressed in conspicuous consumption become minimum needs, with constantly increased pressure on our halakhhic and spiritual defenses against the *yetzer hara* of wealth. Isaiah's lament about the daughters of Zion and their "tinkling ornaments . . . chains and the bracelets . . . and the bonnets and the headbands and the earrings . . . and the changeable suits of apparel . . . and the mantles and the wimples . . . and the fine linen . . . and the hoods and the veils" (3:18–23) reflects a pattern of never enough. "More is better than less" leads people to strive to increase their equity even though they already possess enough to support themselves, their children, and their children's children. The striving may be motivated by a search for power, communal status, and even philanthropy. But the unlimited nature of the economic *yetzer hara*, despite its legitimacy as a method of satisfying needs, all too often becomes the motivation, hidden or acknowledged, behind economic immorality, fraud, and oppression.

The words of the Chafetz Chaim (leader, teacher, and moralist of Eastern European Jewry before World War II) clarify the cause and effect of patterns of consumption. "One of the reasons for the sin of theft which people do is the [unjustified] expenditure and the [modish] clothing which has become, through our manifold sins, commonplace. These cause all the suffering and tragedies which plague us, both internally and externally. . . . In the beginning the Holy One blessed be He in His Mercy, provides a person with the wherewithal to support his soul, pay his debts to God through charity, *gemilat chesed*, support of Torah scholarship, and so on. However, soon the *yetzer hara* entices him to conduct his household affairs, clothing, and so forth, in a fashion far above his means, so that he will achieve social status. . . . Then when his income is insufficient to achieve or to maintain such a standard of living . . . he succumbs to theft, to robbery, to fraud and to evade his debts" (*Sefer Tamim*, chap. 5).

The immoral effect of blurring the distinction between needs and wants is multiplied by the ease with which we are able to rationalize our unethical actions. Our sages taught that "most people are guilty of dishonesty" [as distinct from murder and violence], and Rashi explains that this is because they allow themselves to prevent their fellows from profiting from their commerce (*Talmud Bavli*, *Bava Basra* 165a). Continuing in the same vein, Shmuel Chaim Luzzatto (18th-century moralist) writes that "In their business dealings most people get a taste for stealing, whenever they permit themselves to make an unfair profit at the expense of somebody else, claiming that such profits are not theft. So it is not merely obvious and explicit theft which needs to concern us, but any unethical transfer of wealth that may occur in ordinary and everyday economic activity" (*Mesillat Yesharim*, chap. 21).

Unscrupulous business deals, the exploitation of ignorance or need, and the use of false or even dishonestly suggestive advertising are examples of both Rashi's and Luzzatto's thinking. The growth of depersonalized economic institutions and large national or multinational corporations facilitates this rationalization of unethical business behavior. In the same way, the rationalizing is strengthened by the economic relationships between individuals and government authorities at all levels. Exploitation of welfare entitlements, the abuse of subsidies and of government aid to development, and tax evasion hardly seem like *aveirot* at all. Employee pilfering and private use of employers' facilities and materials are often viewed casually, as no more than "crimes" against the depersonalized corporation. The same rationalization enables us to make excessive claims from insurance companies or to transfer rights to others who are not entitled to them or to illegally use frequent flyer credits earned by the corporate employer for our own personal benefit.

The gradual growth of the corporate concept from a means of limiting shareholders' liabilities to creditors into the creation of a separate moral identity is a further factor. This phenomenon affects corporations of all sizes, listed or not, whether owner managed or directed by nonshareholder officers. Such an independent corporate ethical personality allows shareholders to absolve themselves from any non-halakhic or immoral actions of the corporation. In the same way, directors use the corporate veil to justify unethical behavior in the pursuit of maximizing profits for their shareholders. There does seem to be a place in *halakhah* for a form of business organization whereby the liabilities of the shareholders are limited to the amount of equity they own (Menashe Klein, *Mishneh Halakhot*, pt. 6, sec. 277). However, almost all authorities hold that Jews cannot evade the obligations the Torah places on the possession of wealth by transferring it to a limited liability corporation. This we see in the decisions about *chametz* owned by a corporation with Jewish shareholders (*Elef LeShlomo*, sec. 238), regarding interest extended by a Jewish mortgage bank (*Minchat Yitzchak*, pt. 3, sec. 1; pt. 4, sec. 16) and *Shabbat* (*Iggrot Moshe, Orach Chaim*, pt. 1, sec. 62).

In order to keep away from *aveirot* of wealth, business, and consumption one needs a lifestyle of "enough" and an awareness of the wide, all pervasive, and all inclusive halakhic framework within which Jews are required to operate.

Positive and Negative Commandments—*Mitzvot Asei* and *Mitzvot Lo Ta'aseh*

Knowledge of the halakhic framework and adherence to it are the only ways to curb the rationalizing that eases economic immorality and the power of unsatisfied wants. Study shows that this framework goes far beyond simple and clear questions of robbery to include every aspect of business activity and every item of expenditure. Almost all this framework applies equally to men and women, with no distinction between laymen, rabbis, and unlearned Jews. Furthermore, this framework is an integral part of Judaism, the result of a Divinely revealed Torah, not merely another example of human legislation. It is true that the *mishpatim*—judgments—seem to have a raison d'être that is obvious and easily understood—mainly the peaceful and harmonious legal system without which neither business, economics, nor any social activity can exist. However, the truth is that *mishpatim*—the civil, criminal, and social framework of Torah—together with the *eidot* and *chukim* form a whole. Thus economic immorality and sins between man and man are, additionally, sins against the God who commanded the *mishpatim*.

The Psalmist sings, "The beginning of Your word is truth and Your just commandments are forever" (Psalm 119). Rava explained that from the end of the Ten Commandments—*mitzvot* between man and man—we learn the truth of the first commandments between man and God. Rashi, quoting the *Midrash*, tells us that the nations of the world complained that the Lord gave His commandments for His own glorification. Later, on hearing the social commandments, they confessed that the beginning was perfect truth (*Talmud Bavli*, *Kiddushin* 31a).

"The nations of the world think that God commanded the rational *mitzvot* because they are a self-evident and logical truth. Israel, however, says, 'You are a God of Truth and there is no other truth.' Therefore one may not steal because the God of truth forbade it, and one may not rob because He said so; and thereby this injunction becomes truth" (the Admor Kalonymos of Pishiasetzana, who perished in the Warsaw Ghetto).

"There are, in the Torah, *eidot*, which bear witness to the presence of God and to His great wonders such as the Sabbath, the unleavened bread on Pesach, and the Festival of Sukkot. The reason for these is clearly to be a memorial of His wondrous acts. There are also *chukim*—laws [such as the Red Heifer, *sha'atnez* (mingling of diverse fibers), *tzitzit*] the reasons and rationale for which are hidden from us. Therefore we view them as Divine edicts. In both these cases it is easy to see and understand the difference between Divinely revealed Judaism and other religions. . . . However, the difference between *mishpatim*, the Torah judgments between man and man, and the human legislation and social contract of other religions or societies is often not understood or realized. Yet the psalmist sings 'His statutes and judgments [He related] to Israel. He did not do so for any other nation, and such judgments, they know them not' (Psalm 147:19–20). . . . In *Shemot Rabbah* they said that Moses said to Israel, 'Behold God gave you His Torah, if you do not keep the *dinim* [between man and man] He will take back the Torah.' Why? Because He only gave you the Torah in order that you should keep His *dinim* as it is written, 'The power of the King is the Justice which He loves' . . . this includes the laws of finding lost articles and the [business] actions of people." (Abarbanel, *Introduction to Exodus* 21).

Abarbanel goes on to show two main differences between these Divine judgments and the business or economic regulations, legislation, and structure within which all other societies and nations operate. The Torah expands the concepts of economic morality and business ethics far beyond the grasp of human intelligence. Furthermore, the Torah's insistence on Divine reward and punishment ensures that people know there is no possibility of the secret crimes or hidden actions that constitute white collar crime, injustice, and exploitation.

"All the monetary laws obligatory on Jews are forbidden to Noachides as well, under the injunction against theft. These include the laws of theft [not to steal money or possessions; to have a '*bet din*' that judges and punishes thieves; to consistently see that one has true weights and measures for solids and liquids; not to do injustice with weights and measures; not even to possess defective weights and measures; not to encroach on a neighbor's property (*hasagat g'vul*, understood to include competition that deprives another of his livelihood); not to steal humans and sell them (*Mishneh Torah*, Introduction to *Hilkhot Geneivah*)] robbery [not to forcefully take another's property, even a debt owed to one; not to oppress somebody by denying a debt or to abuse a trust fund or a deposit or to withhold wages or even by badgering and pressing them to legally sell something which the seller does not wish to sell; not to covet people's standard of living, which is so often the root cause of fraud and theft; to return what was robbed; not to ignore a lost article; to return a lost article, which in both negative and positive forms applies to the protection of people's possessions from loss through other people's plotting or conniving (*Mishneh Torah, Introduction to Hilkhot Gezeilah*)]; *onaah*—price fraud through overcharging [both in relation to the market price and as a percentage of costs]; oppression and withholding wages [actually there is also an obligation to pay on time]; not to prevent a worker from eating of the produce he is working with but not with gluttony nor transfer it (this would seem to apply to benefits provided by modern labor relations); not to muzzle an animal during its working to prevent it from eating at the same time (it is meritorious to muzzle the animal so as not to eat of another's produce)]; the obligations of bailies [*din shomrim*, relating to a person's degree of responsibility for property entrusted to him in various capacities, as agents, craftsmen, chief executive officers, and certain classes of employees]; damages to property or to person [not only physical damage but also causing another financial loss. If a person damages another's property, the payment of the damage brings atonement but it requires appeasement of the injured person for his bodily damages before one can be forgiven. Furthermore, a person must prevent damage caused by his property or person to another, including removal of dangerous objects from the public thoroughfare]; laws of borrowing and lending [to make interest-free loans, both to the poor and to the rich; not to oppress debtors by vigorously demanding repayment from one who cannot pay; not to secure debt through coercion; to return an essential article, which serves as security, whenever the borrower requires it; not to delay this return; not to demand a lien from a widow; not to insist on tools or equipment required for sustenance; not to lend money at interest nor to serve as an agent for such a transaction nor as a witness nor as a scribe nor as a surety (*Mishneh Torah*, *Introduction to Hilkhot Malveh Ve'Loveh*)]; laws of buying and selling [not to defraud in buying or selling by false advertising or nondisclosure of defects or to create an illusion that the goods or services produce status or other desired but irrelevant effects]" (*Ramban*, *Genesis* 34:14).

This extended concept of theft, dishonesty, oppression, and economic morality is, as Abarbanel mentioned, only one characteristic of the *mishpatim*. In addition there is Divine reward and punishment for observance of these laws; this presupposes the Divine cognizance of people's most secret and private actions. Most white collar crimes, economic oppression, fraud, and abuse of our fellowman are carried out in secret, in the dark nooks and crannies of society; this awareness ultimately provides the policing of our actions.

See how Torah resounds with this constant awareness of God, especially in those actions between man and man, where God becomes the eternal witness, judge, and executor of appropriate punishment.

"You shall not oppress any widow or orphan. If you afflict them in any way, they will surely cry out to Me and I shall surely hear them. And my anger will be exceedingly great and I will kill you with the sword and your wives shall be widows and your children orphans" (Exodus 22:21–23).

"And you shall not glean your vineyard, neither shall you gather every grape of your vineyard; you shall leave them for the poor and the stranger; I am the Lord God."

"You shall not curse the deaf nor put a stumbling block before the blind, but shall fear your God"

"You shall love your neighbor as yourself; I am the Lord."

"You shall not vex [oppress] the stranger . . . you shall love him as yourself; for you were strangers in the Land of Egypt; I am the Lord your God."

"You shall do no unrighteousness in judgment in measures, in weight and in liquid measure. Just weights, just balances, just measurements and just measures, shall you have. I am the Lord your God which brought you out of the land of Egypt [The linkage between the Exodus and the laws of weights and measures flows from the fact that He who distinguished between the seed of a firstborn and others, the most private knowledge imaginable, will surely punish he who soaks his weights or falsifies his measures in secret in order to defraud" (*Talmud Bavli*, *Bava Metziah* 61b)] (Leviticus 19).

"Rabbi Shimon the son of Rabbi Yehuda HaNasi [redactor of the *Mishnah* c. 250 C.E.] says the biblical verse in Deuteronomy 12:16 warns, you shall surely strengthen your heart against eating the blood [of animals slaughtered for food] because the blood is the soul." [Avoiding drinking] blood, [something] which the soul of people view with repulsion, nevertheless earns one Divine reward. Economic immorality and sexual immorality for both of which the soul of man lusts and covets, one who separates himself from them will surely earn Divine reward for himself, his children and descendants until the end of the generations" (*Talmud Bavli*, *Makkot* 23b).

The Baal Shem Tov was once riding on a wagon when the carter asked him to keep watch while he stopped to cut hay for his horse from one of the adjoining fields. No sooner had he entered the field when the Baal Shem Tov started to shout, "They see, they see." Hurriedly the man climbed back on the wagon, looked around in fear, and said, "But there's nobody around to see." "You forget," said the Baal Shem Tov, pointing heavenward, "there is always One who sees." An echo of Abraham's answer to Avimelech, king of the Philistines, who asked why Abraham suspected them of being capable of adultery and murder. "I know that there is no fear of God in this place" (Genesis 20:11).

A *shochet*, "ritual slaughterer," once came to the Chafetz Chaim for advice, saying, "The laws of *shechitah* are so many and difficult I am afraid that I may sin and cause others to sin through an infringement of them. I think I will go into business." The Chafetz Chaim's reply was simple and direct: "If your major concern is the safety of your soul, you should remain a *shochet*. The laws of the marketplace and of money are far more numerous and onerous, while God, your partner, is an ever-present witness and judge to any deviations."

The culmination of the halakhic and moral dimensions of the Jewish perspective on wealth is the creation of a *talmid chakham*—an economic man. Here righteousness and modesty merge to create a form of business conduct and lifestyle that has been a role model for Jews for centuries in all the countries of their dispersion.

"The *talmid chakham* provides for his family according to his means, yet without excessive devotion to this pursuit ['You shall walk modestly before your God,' the spiritual demand of Amos the prophet, calls for simplicity in consumption, dress, and furniture. So] clothing should be neither that of kings nor that of poor men, but rather pleasant, ordinary clothing. The Torah scholar should eat his normal meals in his own house and should not participate in public feasting, even with scholars. It is fitting for him to eat in public [which is more expensive and conspicuous] only those meals associated with a religious precept, such as the marriage of a scholar to the daughter of a scholar.

"The Jewish role model for commerce has to act in truth and in faith. His *yes* is to be yes and his *no*, no. He forces himself to be exact in calculations when he is paying but is willing to be lenient when others are his debtors. He should not buy on credit when he has the wherewithal to pay cash nor should he be surety for a loan [getting involved in potential conflicts that are not of his concern] or serve as a representative to collect others' debts. [This does not refer to acts of charity or to assisting in collecting debts from recalcitrant debtors.] He should keep his obligations in commerce, even when the law permits him to withdraw or retract, so that his word is his bond; but if others have obligations to him he should deal mercifully, forgiving and extending credit. He should be careful not to deprive his neighbor of his livelihood [even where this is legal] or cause hardship and anguish to others [either bodily or financially]. He who acts in this way is the one referred to by the prophet Isaiah, when he said in God's Name, 'You are My servant, Israel, in whom I exalt'" (*Mishneh Torah*, *Hilkhot De'ot* 5:13).

Consequences of Immorality and Sin in Matters between Man and Man

God's judgment always fits the crime; *midah k'neged midah*, the greater the sin, the greater the punishment. Throughout the history of the Jewish people and of mankind in general, economic dishonesty, exploitation, and material egoism have been the ultimate causes of Divine retribution.

Adam and Eve's sin was theft—taking that which did not belong to them—and so they were expelled from the Garden of Eden.

"The fate of the generation of the Flood was only sealed because of theft" (*Talmud Bavli, Sanhedrin* 108b). Actually, the biblical verse tells us that "the earth became filled with *chamas*, 'wrongdoing.'" *Chamas* halakhically refers to the theft of something less than a *shaveh prutah*, only of marginal worth. In the modern world, such acts are not usually considered criminal—exploiting expense accounts, exploiting consumer ignorance, slight overcharging, withholding due payments to benefit from short-term inflationary price charges. "Society is able to control robbery and theft through police work and jails but by *chamas*, 'underhand dealing,' by cunning, by astute dishonesty, by craftily keeping within the letter of the Law, it goes to ruin; by [those] wrongs which human justice cannot reach but which can only be prevented by self-judging consciousness before God" (Samson Raphael Hirsch on Genesis 6:11). The Admor of Sochochow comments in the same vein that although the generation of the Flood committed all three cardinal sins—idolatry, murder, and sexual immorality—their fate was sealed through the theft that causes all the social and spiritual fabric to unravel (Shem MiShmuel, *Parshat Noach*).

"And the people of Sodom were exceedingly evil and sinful before God (Genesis 13:13). *Sinful* refers to their monetary sins as it is written, 'and it will be a sin for you' (Deuteronomy 23:21), referring to one who delays payment of an oath or withholds the wages of a worker" (*Talmud Bavli, Sanhedrin* 109a).

Avot d'Rabbenu Natan tells us, "Hakadosh Baruch Hu did not destroy the generation of the Tower of Babel although they rebelled against Him, because they loved [cared and dealt fairly with each other]; He only dispersed them. However, the people of Sodom were destroyed both in this world and for the world to come, because they hated each other, even as it is written, 'they were exceedingly evil' to each other" (*Pirkei Avot d'Rabbenu Natan*, chap. 12). In contrast to Sodom's destruction for social misdeeds, God blesses Abraham in *Parshat Vayeira* (chap. 18:18–19) "because he will teach his children to do acts of charity [meaning acting *lifnim mishurat hadin*, waiving one's legal rights in business (*Talmud Bavli*, *Chullin* 134b)] and justice."

Rashi links the punishment for false weights and measures to the enemies plaguing the Jews when he explains the proximity of weights and measures to the injunction to remember what Amalek did to us (Deuteronomy 25:17). Isaiah, Jeremiah, Ezekiel, and indeed all the prophets link the destruction of Israel to immoral social behavior as well as idolatry. Amos echoes all the prophetic books when he proclaims, "For three sins of Israel and for four I will not forgive them. In that they sold the righteous for silver [bribery, which leads the judges to punish the innocent, similar to the idea expressed in Exodus 23:7] and the poor for a pair of shoes, [even for the slight gain of a pair of shoes, or defrauding them even of their shoes. The Hebrew word for shoe is *na'al*, which means to close or lock in. This prompts Rashi to explain that the rich oppressed the poor and bought up their fields scattered amongst those of the rich so that ultimately the latter had a large continuous area that prevented the entry of others; an act that was legal but condemned by the prophet]. They pant after the dust of the poor [oppressing and humiliating them so that the dust covers their heads] and distort the way of the humble [forcing them into corrupt ways as an escape from oppression] . . . and they [the rich] lay themselves on couches, covered with pledged garments [given to creditors as surety for loans but needing to be returned whenever needed by the poor] in festive meals [*seudot mitzvah*] before the altars" (Amos 2:7–8).

The foreboding of the prophets was realized in the expulsion of the Ten Northern Tribes and later in Nebuchadnezzar's destruction of the Temple in Jerusalem. Then, almost 2,000 years ago, the Second Temple was destroyed by the Roman emperor Titus, national independence was lost, and the long Jewish exile began. Inter alia these misfortunes occurred because of the love of wealth; this in turn caused oppression, social dishonor, and economic suffering (*Talmud Yerushalmi*, *Yoma*, chap. 1, *halakhah* 1). The Babylonian Talmud saw this destruction as being the result of the strict insistence on obtaining all legal rights in property, business transactions, and creditor–debtor relationships (*Bava Metziah* 30b).

Not only does punishment flow from business and economic action but so does salvation as well. The rabbis (*Talmud Bavli*, *Shabbat* 31a) called the mishnaic tractate of *Nezikin* (literally, "damages," but actually the earliest codification of Jewish business, civil, and criminal law) by an alternate name—The Book of Salvation. Rabbi Yehuda HaNasi cited the *Pirkei Avot*, the only moral and ethical portion of his *Mishnah*, at the end of this order. Redemption through business behavior and material righteousness occurs not only at the individual level but also at the cosmic one. This is a constant theme, not only of the books of the Bible but also of the prophetic writings and rabbinic literature, even including that of a halakhic nature.

On *Shabbat Chazon*, preceding *Tisha B'Av*, the anniversary of the destruction of both Temples in Jerusalem and the beginning of the exile, we read the prophetic portion from the first chapter of Isaiah. The prophet ends his dirge saying, "Zion will be redeemed by Justice and her returnees by Righteousness" (Isaiah 1:28).

Rabbi Moshe of Coucy, writing in thirteenth-century. Franco-Germany, authored a compendium of laws entitled *Sefer Mitzvot*

Gadol. He, like the authors of similar compendiums, added moral insights to his legal opinions. Regarding the obligation of returning lost articles (Exodus 23:4; Deuteronomy 50:1–3), he wrote:

"I have already expounded both in the exile of Spain and the exiles of the Edomites that because our exile has been excessively prolonged, Israel should separate themselves from the vanities of the world while identifying themselves with the Truth that is the seal of God. Neither should they deal falsely with other Jews nor with non-Jews nor defraud them in any way. Rather they should sanctify themselves even in those [economic and commercial] acts which are [legitimate and] permitted to them; even as it is written, 'and the remnant of Israel shall neither do evil nor defraud in speech, nor shall there be found on their lips deceit.' [Then] when the Holy One blessed be He will come to redeem us, the nations of the world will declare 'in justice does He redeem them since they are people of truth and the law of truth is on their lips.' However, if their dealings are false, then the nations will say, 'the Holy One blessed be He deals unjustly in that He chose as His portion thieves and deceivers' [and so Divine Justice will demand a continuation of the exile]" (*Sefer Mitzvot Gadol, Hilkhot Hashavat Aveidah*, p. 152b).

3

VIDUY—CONFESSION

The confession of sins is the centerpiece of the entire worship of Yom Kippur—the Day of Atonement—and is repeated in all the different services of that day. There are actually two series of confessions, each with its different characteristics and content. These are the *Ashamnu* prayer and the longer *Al Chet*.

Ashamnu consists of an alphabetically arranged list of sins corresponding to the twenty-two letters of the Hebrew alphabet. It is recited both in the silent *amida* even in the *mincha* service of Yom Kippur eve and in the reader's repetition on that day, when it is chanted in unison. This *Ashamnu*, however, is a general confession—"We have become guilty, we have betrayed . . ."—without a detailed description of the sins involved. The recitation of *Ashamnu* is not limited to Yom Kippur, but is mandatory on all fast days, including that of the bride and bridegroom on the afternoon of their wedding. It is also part of the *selichot*, penitential prayers that precede Rosh Hashanah and are included on the days between that holy day and Yom Kippur. Furthermore, the Sepharadi order of prayers and that of the chasidic groups include this confession in the penitential prayers recited daily.

The longer *Al Chet*, which is restricted to Yom Kippur, is a detailed list of types of sins, also arranged in alphabetical order but with two verses for each letter: a total of forty-four verses. These verses are not said aloud but represent a private confession; the cantor's repetition of the last verses of each section seems to be an organizational rather than a theological arrangement. However, the public chanting of "For all these" between three groups of the *Al Chet* is of deliberate spiritual significance. Although it is customary to recite the *Al Chet* humbly and bowed, "For all of these" is sung joyously while standing erect. After quietly reviewing our sins, expressing contriteness for them, and avowing by the recitation not to repeat these acts, we are assured of God's forgiveness. The Hebrew terms express different stages of forgiveness: *Slicha*—"forgive"—relates to the total forgiveness of the sin; *mechila* relates to the punishment—a complete waiver even though the sin itself has not been forgiven; and *kapparah* refers to the temporary suspension of the punishment. The aspect of forgiveness applicable is related to the enormity of the crime and the degree of penitence. In response to this mercy and love we are able to publicly and in unison sing out, after confession, "For all of these, O God of forgiveness, forgive us, pardon us, atone for us." With the same faith, the concluding prayer of Yom Kippur, *Neilah* , does not include the *Al Chet*. Rather there is the constant repetition of the Thirteen Attributes of God's mercy and the structuring of most of this service around these expressions of His mercy and forgiveness. When all is said and done, after the repetitive confessions of the day and when we stand weakened from the fast, the ultimate forgiveness is from His mercy.

The confessions are all couched in the plural form. This is characteristic of almost all Jewish prayer, an expression of the communal and national orientation of Judaism. One perhaps expects, however, the *Al Chet* to be phrased in the singular, after all, each person is obligated to consider and confess his own individual sins. More important, the communal form may tend to make the recitation of the *Al Chet* mechanical and meaningless. Although both these observations contain degrees of truth, the plural form is essential to the very nature of the confession. While this is the case in all aspects of life, the plural is specifically inherent in the earning and spending of money, because of the social nature intrinsic to the interplay of market forces, the determination of consumption patterns, and the conceived role of growth. Here all acts of individuals flow from the surrounding ethical culture within which the individual operates and the socio-economic forces. Our personal accountability for our actions is not blunted, but individual responsibility is extended beyond our own sins. We must also participate in others' responsibilities. When individuals do not repudiate fraudulent business acts by members of their communities, when they do not hold the perpetrators accountable, or use social and religious pressure to punish them, then all become partners in the perpetrators' crimes.

"One who has the ability to protest but does not, the sin is ascribed to him" (Ramah, *Shulchan Arukh, Yoreh De'ah*, sec. 334, subsec. 48). These words echo the *Yalkut Shimoni* on *Shoftim*, which tells us, "Pinchas killed (as it were) all those who died in the war against the tribe of Benjamin. He had the power as the priest to protest, but did not. The Sanhedrin should have tied even ropes about their waists and gone through all the cities of Israel to teach them proper behavior."

Not only does the obligation of protest make everybody a party to the white collar crime, fraud, and exploitation; ultimately without it society must crumble. "Jerusalem was destroyed," said the rabbis in the Talmud (*Shabbat* 1991a), "because they did not admonish one another." It must be stressed that a society cannot be moral in some aspects, for instance, sexual, and immoral in others, for example, economics. The lack of public awareness and criticism in business morality leads easily from an individual's white collar crime to an all-pervasive corruption. First the acts are condoned, shoulders are shrugged, and even admiration expressed for the cleverness and shrewdness behind the sharp business deals, tax evasion, and fraud. This condoning climate creates a permissive culture until these unhalakhic and immoral acts become normal and acceptable. Then the originally innocent people lose sight of their values and no longer have clear-cut guidelines for their economic, business, and social actions. "Everybody does it" becomes acceptable, and corruption is a fact.

The communal character of the *Al Chet* not only invokes the obligation of protesting economic immorality, it also reflects the national-social character of Judaism, as contrasted with the individual ego orientation of other religions. The aim to create a nation of priests and a holy people establishes social responsibility, charity, and economic justice as constant requirements for communal living, at individual and communal levels.

Jews are responsible not only for the physical and religious well-being of their fellows, but also for their economic welfare, security, and success. The rabbis interpret the dual meaning of the Hebrew phrase *damim*—literally, "blood," but also "money"—to rule that "if one knows that others are plotting to cause another financial harm, he is required to tell him [so that he can protect himself] even as it is written: 'and you shall not stand on your brother's blood'" (*Shulchan Arukh, Choshen Mishpat*, sec. 426, subsec. 1).

This rule is considered an application of the obligation to return lost goods, preventing financial loss being the same as returning the found article. "One who does not return a found article, intending to keep it for himself, is considered a robber" (*Mishneh Torah, Hilkhot Gezeilah*, chap. 11, *halakhah* 2). "One who ignores the lost article transgresses" (chap. 11, *halakhah* 1). The rule also applies to passing on information about reliability of services rendered or of goods supplied to prospective buyers. The sophistication of the services or goods is not relevant, so that information regarding craftsmen, and professionals or takeovers and financial reports all seem to come under this obligation. "One cannot hide behind the fear of talking *lashon hara*—talebearing—to evade this responsibility" (*Chafetz Chaim, Shmirat HaLashon, Klall Yud*).

Important as the individual obligation to protest and inform against business immorality are the obligations of the rabbinic courts in these matters. These include the judicial role of considering cases of business dishonesty and punishing the culprits. However, there is also the obligation on the *bet din* both to intervene in the marketplace and to force members of the community to fulfill the social and moral obligations placed on them by the community. It is often argued that in the open societies in which Jews live today these extended obligations of the *batei din* cannot be met. In this regard, historical evidence over the centuries shows that the only enforcement powers rabbinic courts always had was their use of social, religious and moral peer pressure, a pressure that exists even today.

"The *bet din* may force one to act in business unselfishly—*midat sodom*, the attribute of the people of *Sodom*." Some authorities hold that means physical coercion, while others hold that this only means social or religious pressure (*Teshuvot HaTzemach Tzedek, Choshen Mishpat*, sec. 23). These attributes refer to competition that destroys the livelihood of others, forestalling another in business negotiations (*ani mehapech be chararah*), or demanding payment when one knows the debtor cannot pay (here the waiving of the creditor's rights is only an act of charity).

The *bet din*'s more prosaic function of adjudicating financial matters and punishing the transgressors (which includes those who refuse to appear before the rabbinic court or to obey their decisions) is simply proof that fraud, oppression, and dishonesty are all crimes against God and need to be treated as such. Otherwise, recourse could simply be made to a civil authority devoid of any spiritual or religious significance.

Chillul Hashem

"One who desecrates the Holy Name [through his actions] is never granted full forgiveness until he dies. This is so even though he repented properly [during his lifetime], even though Yom Kippur has passed [which normally brings forgiveness if one has repented], and even though the sinner has suffered serious pain and tribulations [which usually bring forgiveness even for the most serious crimes]" (*Mishneh Torah, Hilkhot Teshuvah*, chap. 1, *halakhah* 4).

4

בְּאִמּוּץ הַלֵּב

B'imutz Halev—By Acting Callously

We act callously and insensitively when we disregard or even turn our backs on the needs of the distressed and disadvantaged in our community. A Jew is expected to allocate at least 10 percent of his earnings to charitable purposes, and we act callously when we withhold that part of our earnings, which was given to us for that purpose. Shaming of staff or peers in front of others and any harassment or bullying behavior in the office would also be forms of callousness. Literally, *imutz halev* means strengthening one's heart to kill the feelings of human kindness. In our desire to keep all our legally earned wealth solely for our own selfish needs, we emotionally and rationally harden our hearts to justify our selfishness and ignore the needs and sufferings of others. That same strength also causes others sorrow by ignoring their feelings or their psychological needs.

Charity as the Antidote for the Callous Heart

What feeds this selfish strengthening is our fear that we cannot afford to give charity, or to assist in action and in words the disadvantaged or the sufferers, or to deal kindly with others. It is a resentment against sharing what legally belongs to us with others and thereby having less to use for our own needs. Naturally, nobody is willing to *admit* to this resentment, so the ever-fertile human imagination finds numerous rationalizations to make the hardened heart seem less despicable or more reasonable.

Turnos Rufus, a Roman governor in *mishnaic* Israel, explained to Rabbi Akiva that since "this person is poor because he lacks merit or is not deserving, so the Holy One hates him, and I will not support him by giving him charity" (*Talmud Bavli*, *Bava Basra* 10a).

Christianity developed this distinction between deserving and nondeserving poor, which Judaism does not accept. The reasons for the person's poverty, his ability to effectively change his situation, or the evaluation by the giver of alternative methods of assisting him are never allowed to become factors absolving the Jew of his obligation to help.

One who borrowed money from gentiles and fraudulently denied payment was imprisoned for his debt. Is the community obligated to ransom him using charity funds even though his imprisonment is his own fault? The halakhic answer is simple and clear—yes. Furthermore, Maimonides explicitly rules that if he repeats his fraud, he still receives the communal assistance. It is only when it is repeated again that the obligation ceases. If there is danger to his life in prison, however, the necessity of saving his life takes precedence over his self-created guilt (*Mishneh Torah*, *Matnot Aniyim*, chap. 8, *halakhah* 13).

In our own day, the Chief Rabbi of Tel Aviv, Rabbi Chaim David HaLevy, ruled similarly in the case of a poor person who smokes; presumably the same could apply to other forms of addiction.

"You ask if it is a *mitzvah* to give charity to a poor person who smokes, since he spends this money on things that damage his health [something forbidden under Jewish law since we are commanded to be exceedingly careful to guard ourselves against physical harm]. Perhaps without our charity he would refrain from smoking even against his will. It seems to me that it is absolutely clear that one may not refrain from giving him charity . . . even if he is aware of the dangers inherent in smoking but is unable to give it up . . . he cannot be made hungry because of that [just as we may not apply a means test regarding one who requires food." Rabbi Isser Meltzer, one of the leading Jerusalem rabbis of the last generation, opened his door to whosoever knocked on it, reechoing the "you shall surely open" of Deuteronomy 15.8. Once when he was ill, one of his students, hearing a knock, asked, "Who is it?" "What," came the rabbi's voice from his bed, "somebody is standing outside on a cold winter's night after midnight, and all you can do is ask,'Who is it?' Open the door"]. "This obligation to provide charity to the smokers can be deduced from the case of a poor person who is lax about religious observance; who does not say blessings nor wash his hands before meals, and so on. Even though one is not permitted to give him food, if he is poor we are commanded to sustain him and give him food by the laws of charity" (*Asei Lecha Rav*, vol. 5, p. 375).

The fact that some people pretend poverty while others use different fraudulent acts to persuade us to give them charity is another popular rationalization for hardening our hearts. Halakhically we are not obligated to give charity to frauds and are entitled to examine the economic situation of those approaching us, except if a life is in danger. At the same time we must guard against using the possibility of fraud in order to simply evade giving charity.

In the modern open societies in which we live, however, as often as not people defraud the state-funded welfare funds, food stamps, and tuition subsidies by claiming poverty in order to become eligible. State loans, tariffs, fiscal benefits to promote employment are features of many modern economies and lend themselves to abuse by entrepreneurs, who then benefit from public funds. The rationale here is the public, impersonal nature of the funds, which helps people pretend that welfare fraud is not really fraud. Halakhically, stealing from the public is far worse than stealing from individuals, since one cannot do real *teshuvah*. After all, it is impossible to identify the taxpayers from whom the welfare money was stolen, in order to return the money to them.

The source of this *imutz halev* is the lust for money, and the antidote for the callous heart is charity in all its forms; monetary, spiritual, and physical.

"If there be among you a needy man from among one of your brethren, within any of your gates in the land which God, your God gives you, you shall not harden your heart to make it unfeeling, nor shall you shut your hand from your brother, the needy man. But rather, open wide [literally, 'open, you shall open'] your hand to him; and you shall also lend him [if you cannot give it all to him as a gift] sufficient for all his needs, for what he lacks" (Deuteronomy 15:7,8). To one who cannot decide between his selfishness and his desire to act kindly, God says "You shall not harden your heart." To one who already has decided to deal compassionately with others yet at the last minute is faced with his own ego, the Torah says, "You shall not close your hand" (Rashi).

This teaches us that "it is a positive commandment to give charity to the Jewish poor according to their needs, if you have enough to satisfy them. [The Rama rules that this obligation of satisfaction devolves only on the community, but the individual, nevertheless, has the obligation to bring the needs to the attention of the community], and everyone who sees a poor person asking for help but ignores the plea and does not give him charity transgresses a negative commandment even as it is written 'You shall not make your heart unfeeling nor close up your hand to your brother the poor man' [this is a warning not to behave stingily and ungenerously (*Mitzvot Lo Ta'aseh* 232)]" (*Mishneh Torah, Hilkhot Matnot Aniyim*, chap. 7, *halakhah* 1–2).

"We are obligated to be more careful of the commandment to give charity than in regard to any other positive *mitzvah*. Since it is possible that the poor may die before we give them charity, neglect of this *mitzvah* may lead to bloodshed. Charity is the sign of the Jewish righteous person, the descendant of our father Abraham, even as it is written, 'For I have loved him [Abraham] because he commands his descendants and his household after him, that they keep the way of the Lord, doing charity and justice'" (Genesis 18:19; *Tur, Yoreh De'ah*, sec. 247).

"This duty of caring and providing for the poor rests both on the community and on the individual; it is a demand that cannot be met by the individual or the community separately but requires a joint effort [the individual lacks the financial resources to satisfy these needs yet cannot escape his private obligations. So] the notice affixed to houses, 'No beggars need apply, the owners already subscribe to the communal funds' has not engendered the Jewish spirit which this Jewish law has nourished. . . . You shall not be strong [*imutz*] against your heart, which left to its natural Jewish bent is inclined to benevolence. This inclination can only be overcome by cold, calculating, selfish considerations. Everybody who becomes needy is not at once to apply publicly to the administrator of the public funds, but the friends and relations have first to see what they can do. Only where that does not suffice does the community make up the deficiency. . . . The task of benevolence—*tzedakah* (Genesis 15:6)—is duty in its most eminent sense. He who does not help the poor to the utmost of his power commits a sin and is guilty before God . . . 'and it shall be for you a sin'" (S. R. Hirsch on *Genesis* 15:7–8).

"At the beginning, when a person first starts to give of himself to charity, he has to break the cruelty inside him and transform it into mercy. This is the essence of the giving of charity. If a person is naturally merciful this is not service. Rather the essence of service is to break one's meanness and to change it into mercy" (*Likutei Maharan*, sec. 4).

"In the *Talmud Bavli, Sukkah* 49b, 'Rabbi Elazar says, "Everyone who does charity it is as though he fills the world with loving-kindness. [Therefore] anyone who has mercy on the poor, the Holy One blessed be He will have mercy on him"'" (*Tur, Yoreh De'ah,* sec. 247).

"There is no joy greater and more splendid than making the heart of poor people, orphans, widows, and strangers happy, because the person who makes them happy is like the Divine Presence" (Rambam, *Mishneh Torah, Hilkhot Megillah*, chap. 2:17).

Doing Charity

It is important to note that we do not talk about giving charity but rather "to do charity," the giving of the assistance being only part of the *mitzvah*.

"Though this is a positive *mitzvah* from the Torah, we do not, as is usual in other positive commandments, pronounce a blessing over its performance. This is because in order to pronounce blessings it is required to be happy and at peace with the performance of the *mitzvah*. Charity, however, is usually given without joy, without enthusiasm, and without sincerity" (the chasidic master Mendel Meriminov).

All *mitzvot* require simple faith, excepting these *mitzvot* of charity which require knowledge, namely the knowledge of how to give and do charity. It is the "how" which is the real expression of a person's ability to relax the *imutz halev*.

"He should give charity with a warm and friendly expression, with happiness and with a good heart, and he should mourn with the poor person in his distress and should speak words of consolation to him, and if he gave to him with an angry and harsh countenance, he lost the merit of this *mitzvah*" (*Shulchan Arukh, Yoreh De'ah,* 249).

The Baal Shem Tov taught that "if you perform a good deed but have an ulterior motive, it is better not to do it at all. The only exception is charity. Even though it is not as good as doing it with a pure motive, it is still a good deed, since you sustain the poor no matter what your motive."

"There are eight levels of charity, one above the other. The highest level, above which there is no other, is someone who supports the hand of a Jew who has fallen low, and gives him a gift, a loan, makes him a partner, or finds work for him to support his hand to the point where he is no longer dependent on others. About this it says: 'You shall support him, even the stranger who has become only a sojourner, so that he may live with you.' [That is, support him to the point where he will not fall down again and become needy]" (*Mishneh Torah,*

Hilkhot Matnot Aniyim, chap. 13, *halakhah* 7). This framework described by Maimonides is repeated in the other codes, the *Tur*, and the *Shulchan Arukh*.

The highest level described is particularly pertinent both to modern corporate business and to the Jewish individual as a citizen in the open societies of today. It is a justification for public sector initiatives and macro-economic policies aimed at creating employment for redundant workers, breaking the poverty cycle, and enabling displaced entrepreneurs and workers to establish new businesses. This height of charity places an obligation on corporations to retrain their potentially redundant workers for alternative employment in the changed economic climate, to make available information regarding job opportunities in other companies or areas, and to provide interest-free loans from profits to stimulate entrepreneurship among its displaced workforce. Failing to adopt such corporate strategies or refraining from lobbying and voting for appropriate government policy makes people guilty of *imutz halev*.

The *Sifre* teaches that the compound verb "open your hand," in verse 8, tells us to give again and again and that we are not free of our obligation after giving once or twice. If the poor are too proud to accept our gifts, then we are at least obligated to lend them the money. The same source also provides guidance on the psychological suffering caused by poverty or unemployment. Alleviating a person's financial burden does not remove the mental suffering caused by being told that one is redundant or the depression, crime, and degeneration of prolonged poverty. Financial assistance must provide the comfort and stability of the standard of living enjoyed previously.

Simcha Bunim of Pyscha found it strange that we should be halakhically obligated to provide impoverished people with a horse to ride upon or a servant to go before them if they had previously enjoyed this lifestyle. "The horse, I can understand," he said. "After all, perhaps he is too weak or tired to walk, but the outrider servant I do not understand. This is only a luxurious fantasy. Still," he continued, "we are obligated even to restore this unnecessary foible." The same chasidic master was queried as to why we do not recite a *bracha* before giving charity as is the case in all other positive *mitzvot.* "It's simple," he said, "if we were required to recite a blessing, our piety would lead us to make time-consuming preparations, to attune ourselves spiritually for the performance of this *mitzvah*, and to study all its laws so as to fulfill them properly. After all this, when we come to give the charity, we find the poor have died."

Our methods of doing charitable acts, however, do not affect only the recipients. We ourselves are either enhanced spiritually or suffer religious loss depending on how we perform these acts. "A person should not make a public display of the giving of charity [earning for himself social status and personal pride at the expense of the poor]. If one does show off, not only does he not get merit from God for it, but he is even punished for it" (*Shulchan Arukh, Yoreh De'ah*, 249:13, the gloss of the Rama).

A trustee of charity funds once demonstrated the spiritual effect of his charitable work. "When I first began my communal career, I was unable to eat, drink, or sleep because of the suffering and sorrow I was made to witness. Later I was able to eat and sleep, yet my soul was bothered by the suffering of the poor. As time passed, I was able to live without being bothered. Now, I cannot sleep, drink, or eat without hearing the laments of the poor or the weeping of the suffering people."

Alternative Forms of *Imutz Halev*

Relaxing the *imutz halev* is not achieved only by direct monetary acts. "There is a kind of charity that does not seem to be charity at all but is excellent in God's eyes. For example, a poor person who has an object to sell or a book which people are not keen to buy; when someone buys them from him, there is no greater charity" (*Sefer Chasidim*, sec. 1035).

A poor widow once came to the Admor of Zanz to ask for charity, saying she had used all her money to buy apples but now nobody in the market wanted to buy them. The chasidic master went to the market, and when people saw him selling apples, they thronged to buy them. In a short time, the widow had the money she needed (*Darkhei Chaim*, p. 137).

The hardening of the heart and the resultant arrogance often lead people to oppress others verbally or psychologically. Employers and bureaucrats have great power over their employees or the citizens who require their services. The greater the dependence of the employee or citizen, the greater the potential for exploitation, harassment, and insult. If power corrupts and absolute power corrupts absolutely, it would seem that great economic power is the ultimate corruption. *Halakhah* lays down guidelines that limit the potential for embarrassment and suffering flowing from economic power.

"One may not lend money to a widow, or place a lien, irrespective of whether she is rich or poor [Some commentators explained that the creditor's inspection of his lien would embarrass the widow before her neighbors, while others saw in it a potential for sexual exploitation]" *Mishneh Torah, Hilkhot Malveh U'Loveh*, chap. 3, *halakhah* 1).

Examples of verbal oppression—*onaat devarim*—given by the Codes include reminding a convert of his or her idolatrous past or sinners of their previous errors and transgressions. Even querying prices, goods, or services without an intent to buy sometimes becomes *onaat devarim*. The rabbis saw in the suffixing of "thou shalt fear thy God" to the verse in Leviticus enjoining us from *onaat devarim* the fact that God sees into our hearts where transgression takes place and into the resultant spiritual significance of our acts.

"Rabbi Yochanan said in the name of Rabbi Shimon bar Yochai, 'It is better for a man to cast himself into a fiery furnace than shame his fellow in public'" (*Talmud Bavli, Bava Metziah* 59a).

Obstructing Kindness to Non-Jews

One of the many myths believed in by many Jews and Christians is that non-Jews are not included in the acts of charity and kindness obligatory on Jews. This however is nothing more than a myth and the *imutz halev* of the Jew needs to be weakened in this respect as well.

Non-Jews are obligated, by the Bible's Noachide laws, to have a just and moral legal system, and this seems to include performing acts of charity. Sodom, a gentile city, was destroyed because of the *imutz halev* of its inhabitants, which prevented them from doing acts of mercy and dealing charitably. *Midat Sodom*, this egoistic trait, is seen as being contrary to the Abrahamic family's inheritance of mercy and righteousness. Rabbinic courts have the right to oblige Jews not to act according to *Midat Sodom*.

The inclusion of the non-Jew in the Jew's obligation to break the hardness of his heart applies both to monetary and non-monetary acts of kindness, just as he is obligated in relations with other Jews. Contrary to the halakhic denial of many rights to those who reject their Noachide obligation not to worship idols, charity and kindness include even idolaters.

"One asks after the welfare of the non-Jew [a sign of kindness, using *Shalom*, one of the names of God] because of the demands of peace [even though the idolater rejects God]." The Talmud, discussing the following *mishnah,* expands it beyond the mere inquiry regarding the non-Jew's welfare. "One does not prevent the non-Jewish poor from gathering [the agriculture gifts provided by the Bible for the poor] *leket* (the unharvested stalks of wheat and barley), *shikhakhah* (sheaves left behind in the field) and *peah* (the corners of the field one is obligated to leave unharvested). So, too, one sustains the poor non-Jews with poor Jews because of peace. One visits the non-Jewish sick with the ill Jews. . . . One provides burial for the indigent non-Jew" (*Talmud Bavli, Gittin* 61a). "One eulogizes non-Jews and comforts their mourners" (*Tosefta Gittin*, chap. 3).

All these instances apply not only in those cases where the poor include Jews and non-Jews together (in which case we could assure that the inclusion was meant to prevent jealousy), but also where the non-Jews are a separate entity. This conclusion of the Rashba, the Ran, and the Ritva on the above Talmud passage uses the word *im*, within its connotation of even with; even if sustaining the non-Jews will reduce the amount that can be given to the Jews.

"We support the hands of the non-Jews working their fields during the Sabbatical year. While we are forbidden to do such agricultural work or to assist them physically, we bless them and express our hopes that their efforts will be rewarded" (*Mishneh Torah, Shmittah ve Yovel*, chap. 8, *halakhah* 8).

In view of the potential economic loss incurred through theft or physical damage, "one is obligated to gather [and store in a safe place] the tools and equipment of gentiles [left in the fields]" (*Tur, Shulchan Arukh, Choshen Mishpat*, sec. 266, subsec. 1). "And now [in our day] it is our [Jewish] custom to maintain poor non-Jews with Jews" (*Tur, Shulchan Arukh, Choshen Mishpat*, sec. 249, subsec. 2—Prisha, Bach, Taz, Shach).

"It is also a positive commandment to rise up before the aged [the 'hoary head' of the Divine injunction in Leviticus 20:32], that is, one who is over 70 years (*Mishnah Avot*, chap. 5, *mishnah* 22) [even if he is an idolater, except in the case of an evil person] (Ramah, *Shulchan Arukh, Yoreh De'ah*, sec. 243, subsec. 1).

"Rabbi Yochanan would rise up before aged idolaters, saying 'Look how many years the Holy One blessed be He has granted to them'" (*Talmud Bavli, Kiddushin* 33a).

"When raising communal charitable funds in a town with a mixed Jewish/non-Jewish population [but presumably with an autonomous Jewish council] taxes are collected from Jews and non-Jews alike [even though it is not permitted for Jews to accept charity from non-Jews]" (*Tosefta Gittin*, chap. 3; *Daat Cohen*, sec. 32).

These *halakhot* regarding non-Jews and charity are sometimes said to arise merely from a desire to avoid friction and enmity. There is probably pragmatic justification for this, but it is definitely not the only or even the major ideological factor behind them. This can be clearly seen from Maimonides.

"It is legally permissible to make a gentile slave work rigorously [that is, work at irregular or undefined times, or unnecessary work, the purpose of which is to humiliate or simply to keep the slave busy]. Even though this is legally permissible, nevertheless wisdom and righteousness dictate that a person should be merciful and pursue justice. [One should not therefore] place onerous tasks on the gentile slave nor should one cause him anguish. [One should] give them of all the choice types of food and drink. The early sages would give them the same food and drink which they themselves enjoyed, giving them precedence. [Rabbi Yochanan ate meat and shared it with his gentile slave. He drank wine and shared it with him, saying 'the Lord who created me, created him as well.' This is the quality of righteousness" (*Talmud Yerushalmi, Bava Kamma*, chap. 8, *halakhah* 4)]. So, too, one should not insult them, neither in speech nor in actions; we are permitted to work with them, but not to insult them. One should not scream at them nor talk to them in anger. Rather our speech should be calm and one should pay attention to their complaints. Callousness and arrogance are only to be found amongst idolaters. Israel, the seed of our father Abraham, whom God has revealed to them the righteousness of the Torah and commanded them to observe just laws and edicts—they are merciful to all [after all these] are the characteristics of the Holy One Blessed Be He, which we are commanded to emulate (*Talmud Bavli, Shabbat* 133b, see also *Mishneh Torah Hilkhot De'ot,* chap. 1, *halakhah* 6). As it is written, "and His mercies extend to all his creatures" (Psalms 45:9). The Talmud in *Bava Metziah* 85a includes not only people in this mercy, but also animals. Every person who has mercy on others, God has mercy on them, as it is written, "and allowed you to be merciful and [He will] show mercy unto you and multiply you" (Deuteronomy 13:18)" (*Mishneh Torah, Hilkhot Avadim*, chap. 9, *halakhah* 8).

Postscript

"And the Lord passed before him [Moses] and called out [the 13 attributes of mercy]" (Exodus 34:6).

"Rabbi Yochanan said, 'This teaches that God wrapped himself in a *tallit*, like the *chazzan* who leads the prayers, and showed Moses the order of prayer. He [God] said to him, "whenever Israel sins, let them perform before Me this order and I shall forgive them'" (*Talmud Bavli, Rosh Hashanah* 17b).

Commenting on the verse in Exodus, the Alshich highlights the use of the word "perform" rather than "reciting" in the talmudic passage. This shows that the attributes of God's mercy require that the Jew must perform acts of mercy with others and not only recite the attributes. Then God responds to our prayers with the same kind of mercy.

5

בְּגִלּוּי וּבַסָּתֶר

B'GILUY UVASETER—IN PUBLIC AND IN SECRET

Robbery is obviously committed in public. Far more prevalent, however, are economic crimes conducted in secret, hidden from public scrutiny. Insider trading, exploiting other parties' lack of knowledge about prices, using false weights and measures, deceptive packaging, defective *kashrut* supervision, copying tapes, computer programs, or other protected materials without the knowledge of the owner, and shortchanging are all present-day examples of secret crimes. Buying goods on which no duties or taxes were paid, padding expense accounts, and using an employer's phone for private conversations without permission are all conducted *beseter*.

"A purchasing agent for a firm is offered a commission—bribe?—if he will order goods from a certain supplier. If the goods are inferior or more expensive than those of the competitor, then the agent is guilty of theft. However, if there is no qualitative or price difference, then the agent is required to share the commission with the firm. After all, it is the firm's funds which enable the agent to earn the commission, and one may not have a benefit from another's money without his consent or without paying for it" (*Minchat Tzvi*, pt. 2, sec. 8).

In Secret

"Cursed is he who strikes down his neighbor in secret and all the people shall say 'Amen.'" The Baal HaTurim, commenting on this verse, writes that the numerical value of the Hebrew letters for *beseter*—"in secret"—is the same as that for "he handed over his fellow's money" (Deuteronomy 27:24).

"A person should always be God-fearing (even) in secret admit the truth and speak truth in his heart" (daily morning prayers).

The Admor of Kotsk used to say that while other people performed their righteous deeds in public but their misdeeds in private, he taught his followers to do the opposite. Righteous deeds are to be done privately without spotlight and the misdeeds, performed in public, would be limited by the fear of exposure.

Since Judaism teaches that God is ever-present and all-knowing, there are no secret crimes. It may be possible to act without human knowledge of our misdeeds, but it is quite impossible to act without His knowledge and His punishment. Awareness of this is the major, perhaps the final, resort, the only protection against *b'giluy uvaseter*. The punishment of a thief, one who secretly takes something from someone else, is the payment of a fine of 100 percent (Exodus 22:3). A robber, one who steals openly and in public, must simply return that which he took without a fine.

"Why is the Torah stricter on a thief than on a robber?" queried the Sages. "Because this one [the thief] fears the servant [human beings, and therefore steals in secret] more than the Master: He is not careful about the Eye and Ear above. The

Chillul Hashem—Desecration of God's Name—by the thief is therefore greater than that of the robber" (*Talmud Bavli, Bava Kamma* 79b; see also *Torah Temimah* on Exodus).

"Anyone who does not have mercy on the honor of his Creator, it is fitting that he never came into the world. What is that [not having mercy on the honor of his Creator]? Rabbi Joseph said, 'Someone who sins in private'" (*Talmud Bavli, Kiddushin* 40a).

"You shall not put a stumbling block in the path of the blind, and you shall fear your God" (Leviticus 19:14) [before someone who is blind (ignorant) regarding that thing]. "If someone comes to you for advice, do not give advice that is unsuitable for him [and of which he is ignorant]. Do not say to him 'Sell your field and buy a donkey,' when you wish to buy a field or sell a donkey [through a third party] . . . since only you know the real intention which is in your heart. The verse concludes: 'And you shall fear your God: I am the Lord.' Concerning everything that is secret [literally, a matter of the heart] the Torah says 'and you shall fear God'" (*Sifra, Parshat Kedoshim*, 114.32b).

All who are in the consulting business—accountants, lawyers, stockbrokers, insurance agents, and financial advisers—must be especially wary of placing stumbling blocks secretly in the path of their clients, for example, by hiding possible conflicts of interests. An insurance agent once described how, fearing *b'giluy uvaseter,* he simply let the computer analyze all his clients' data so that the best policy would be offered in light of that data and not his own interest in the commissions and fees offered by various plans or companies.

"Love thy neighbor's well-being as if it were thine own, I am God" (Leviticus 19:18).

"It does not say we are to love the person of our neighbor as we love ourselves, which is practically impossible to carry out. Rather is written *lereacha*—literally 'to your fellowman'—that is, everything which pertains to his person, all the conditions of his life. . . . We are to assist at everything that furthers his [material] well-being and his happiness as if we were working for ourselves and must keep trouble away from him as assiduously as if it threatened ourselves. . . . It follows from 'I am God. . . .' The teachings of honesty, sincerity, truthfulness, faithfulness, caution, justice, consideration of and care for the well-being of others. . . . All these demands for the ordering of our social life are evolved under the divine seal" (S. R. Hirsch on Leviticus 19:18).

This explanation of the linking of God's Name to the social (that is, commercial, economic, and financial activities of people), together with the fear of God's knowledge of all our secret activities, stresses Judaism's consideration of the spiritual effect on the perpetrator, over and above any discussion of the legal consequences.

Weights and Measures

Jewish treatment of weights and measures is a major category of its rejection of secret crimes and its declaration of Divine displeasure with those who perpetrate them.

"Do no wrong in judgment in measures of length, of weight, and of volume. You shall have just scales, just weights, a just *ephah* [a dry measure], and a just *hin* [a liquid measure]. I am God, your God, who brought you out of the land of Egypt" (Leviticus 19:35–36).

Querying the connection between just weights and measures, the rabbis provided two revealing answers. The purpose of the Exodus from Egypt, so basic to Jewish religion and history, was to enable the Jews to observe the laws of just weights. Furthermore, the God who distinguished between the seed of the firstborn who died in Egypt and the other sons, a distinction based on the most intimate and secret knowledge, shall surely punish one who soaks the weights in salt in order to defraud [in secret] (*Talmud Bavli, Bava Metziah* 61b).

"The rabbis taught us that the verse mentions judgment here ['Do no wrong in judgment—measures of length, of weight, and of volume'] because the person who measures is called a judge, and, if he is dishonest in his measure, it is as though he has perverted judgment, and he is called twisted, *meshukatz, cherem* and an abomination. And he causes the five things that are mentioned regarding judges: he defiles the land, profanes the Name of God, causes the Divine Presence to depart, submits the people of Israel to the sword, and banishes them from their land. And the rabbis further enhanced the seriousness of this commandment, saying that its punishment is greater than that for forbidden sexual relations, because this act is between a person and God, while using dishonest weights and measures is between man and his fellow" (*Sefer HaChinukh, mitzvah* 258).

The Law does not frown upon dishonest weights and measures only after they have been used in a fraudulent act (which, as already noted, would be classed as common theft). Rather it views the possession of measures and the act of measuring as legal acts in themselves, so that every measure owned and any material measured out by a Jew become Jewish acts of honesty, symbolic of the Jew's respect for justice and fairness. In this manner the Law establishes the right, per se, in its most absolute form, as a sanctum to be kept inviolate by every Jew and seeks to make the sense of justice, respect for justice, and honesty basic character traits of the Jewish nation (S. R. Hirsch on Leviticus 19:35–36).

"Sometimes a person's evil inclination seduces him in other ways. Saying 'I'm not the only one who does this; there are many people in this town who have deficient weights and measures,' they reduce the amount of goods that they sell, and the purchaser knows nothing of it. By this argument he permits himself to act as they do. In truth, this is a deficiency in belief in Divine Providence, since it is known that the Holy One sustains all the world, and a person's food is allocated to him at the beginning of the year, and the Holy One allocates his sustenance to him through permitted means and not through forbidden means; but the person himself switches it to forbidden means. Therefore, a person has to strengthen his faith in *Hashem* and not weaken. . . . And even if he sees his friends temporarily earning more because of this he should not learn from their actions . . ." (Chafetz Chaim, *Kuntras Middot u'Mishkalot,* footnote).

In Deuteronomy the same laws are repeated in their negative form as well: "That your days may be lengthened in the land which the Lord, your God, gives you. For all that do such things and all that deal unrighteously [here we learn that one may not mix fruit of diverse quality, even newly ripened with older ones (*Sifre*, Deuteronomy 25:18)] are an abomination to God your God" (25:13–16). "The person who transgresses this prohibition and keeps deficient weights in his house, even without using them, he has transgressed" (*Sefer HaChinukh, mitzvah* 602).

"Not only has he done wrong, he is a man whom God has deemed worthy to call Him 'his' God, [but] a Jewish man becomes an abomination of God, his God, if he calls himself a Jew and does not keep what is right and fair. . . . The Jew with a false weight or measure may no longer call God 'his God'" (S. R. Hirsch on Deuteronomy 25:16).

"It is a positive commandment to verify balances, weights, and measures extremely well and to be precise in their calculations" (*Mishneh Torah, Hilkhot Geneivah*, chap. 8, *halakhah* 1).

"One who sells goods deficient in weights and measures, even to a non-Jew, transgresses a negative commandment. You shall not do evil in judgment in weights and measures [in addition to the transgression of you shall not steal]" (*Tur*, *Shulchan Arukh, Hilkhot Onaah u'Mekakh Ta'ut*, sec. 231, subsec. 1).

"He is obligated to return the fraud (*Shulchan Arukh, Baal HaTanya, Hilkhot Middot Vemishkalot*, sec. 2; see also *Mishneh Torah, Hilkhot Geneivah*, chap. 8).

"Even though in other thefts one only transgresses [even though it is still forbidden] when the object has some value, *shaveh prutah*, with regard to the fraud of weights and measures, the Torah was stringent so that one transgresses even with the slightest amount—*mashehu*" (*Sefer HaChinukh, mitzvah* 248, see also the Bach on the *Tur*).

"An idolater too is forbidden to defraud in weights and measures. [This would make it forbidden for a Jew to buy from such a non-Jew since he is putting a stumbling block in the path of the blind.]" (*Minchat Chinukh, mitzvah* 248.)

"The punishment for [defrauding] through weights and measures is very severe, even more than the punishment for sexual immorality. The former is a sin between man and man and the latter between man and God. Fraudulent weights and measures is a denial of the exodus from Egypt" (*Tur, Shulchan Arukh, Choshen Mishpat*, sec. 231, subsec. 19). "The severity of the punishment flows from the fact that one cannot repent properly for the sin of weights and measures. This would require compensating all the defrauded individuals, something which is not possible in view of the large number and anonymity of people involved. So in this case [as in other cases of mass deception such as stock scandals or financial scams] an inferior form of *teshuvah* is proposed, namely the giving of charity or communal service. When one defrauds in this manner, one does so in secret, fearful of exposure or public knowledge. Yet there is no fear of God, and an assumption that God does not see the action of human beings nor does He intervene in them. In the exodus from Egypt, it had become clear to the world that God knows, records, and rewards or punishes all the actions of men" (*Meirat Einayim).*

It is a positive commandment to verify balances, weights, and measures extremely carefully and to be precise in their calculation at the time when they are made.

"Whether he trades with a Jew or a non-Jew, if he undermeasured or underweighed, he has transgressed a negative prohibition and is obligated to return [the money]. It is similarly forbidden to mislead a non-Jew in calculating an account. Rather, he should be precise with him, as the verse says: 'And he will account with his maker,' even though the non-Jew is under his rule, and even more so if he is not. For it comes under the category of 'because it is an abomination to the Lord your God all who act like that, all who behave crookedly'—that is, in any circumstances" (Rambam, *Hilkhot Geneivah,* chap. 8, *halakhah* 1, and end of chap.).

The Talmud records the scrupulous attention paid by Jews in order to save themselves from any doubt or suspicion of defrauding through weights and measures. "The rabbis taught: Abba Shaul the son of Batnit amassed 300 bottles of wine from inexact measurement [of wine when he sold it due to expansion because of heat], and his friends amassed 300 bottles of oil from oil that had clung to the sides of its container when they sold it, and they brought it to the Temple treasurers in Jerusalem. The treasurers said to them: 'You don't need to do this!' They said: 'We do not want this [since the excess really had reduced the quantity sold].' They said to them: 'Since you have been strict on yourselves [regarding just measures], use them for the needs of the general public.'" (*Talmud Bavli, Beitza* 29a).

Price Gouging—*Mafkia Mechirim*

It is interesting to note that the *Shulchan Arukh* and the *Tur* include the injunctions against speculation and price gouging as part of the fraudulent sale—*mekakh t'aut*—as a follow-up to the laws of weights and measures. Indeed this is where they belong. In both false weights and in the fraudulent sale there is an element of secrecy that exploits the ignorance of the other party. Furthermore, in both cases there is a deviation from accepted and known norms. The insistence on unfair pricing practices as a rejection of God's knowledge and punishment is a continuation of the same irreligious behavior about false weights.

"One who raises his prices [above market price or in excess of 'normal profit'] the *Bet Din* has permission to inflict corporal punishment as they see fit. . . . One who exploits the pricing mechanism [of basic goods in times of shortage] or hoards produce [except the primary producer] in the land of Israel or where there is a Jewish majority [even though both are legitimate economic activities] is regarded as a moneylender [who refuses to grant interest-free loans as an act of charity]" (*Tur, Shulchan Arukh, Choshen Mishpat*, sec. 231, subsec. 2 and 25).

False weights and measures defraud through exploiting the assumption by the injured party that common rules are followed. Price gouging exploits exactly the same assumption, and so the *Shulchan Arukh* and the *Arbaah Turim* present the injunctions against it as a follow-up or a corollary to weights and measures.

Theft

"Who is a thief? One who stealthily removes his fellow's money without his knowledge" (*Mishneh Torah, Hilkhot Geneivah VeAveidah*, chap. 1, *halakhah* 3).

"You shall not steal nor deal falsely nor lie one to another (Leviticus 19:11). The verse does not detail which things one should not steal, but simply forbids it. Nothing, not money, not other people's perceptions, and not the perception of God Himself" (Shach).

"Then He said to me, 'This is the curse that goes forth over the face of the whole earth . . . shall enter into the house of the thief and into the house of him that swears falsely by My Name and shall remain in the midst of his house and shall consume it with the timber of it and the stones of it'" (Zechariah 5:3–4). "The verse says 'You shall not steal' (and then the verse says 'You shall not name the name of the Lord your God in vain') (Exodus 19:7). This tells us that anyone who steals ends up making false oaths" (*Mechilta Yitro HaChodesh,* para. 8).

Not only are false oaths and statements made in deceiving through weights and measures, nondisclosure of financial problems, price gouging, and defective goods and services, but they themselves in turn lead to further lies in order to cover up the fraud. Tax evasion is perhaps most virulent in this respect. In order to conceal the evasion one must resort to making false declarations to the tax authorities and to laundering funds either by illegally transferring them to another country or by fraudulently using charitable organizations or legitimate companies. Furthermore, excessive consumption hidden from the eyes of the authorities becomes a major way of using the fraudulently earned tax money. All these actions destroy the moral equilibrium and blur the distinction between right and wrong until lying becomes a way of life in all areas.

"If a person lent money to a debtor on the understanding that he would buy fruit [in order to trade], and he bought utensils, that is forbidden because he misled [literally, 'stole the consciousness'] of the creditor" (*Tosefta Megillah* 1).

"In the whole basketful of human sins theft is the most incriminating" (*Vayikrah Rabbah* 33:3). Stealing from a person is worse than stealing from God. In the first case the fact of one's being a sinner is stated clearly even before he actually commits a wrong (*Talmud Bavli*, *Bava Basra* 81b). These ideas are paralleled by the rabbis, as when Rabbi Yochanan said "Come and see the power of corruption. The generation of the Flood did all the sins and violated everything [adultery, idolatry, and murder]. Yet God's decree against them was only sealed when they stole" (*Talmud Bavli*, *Sanhedrin* 108a).

Though the value of the goods stolen may be trivial, less than a *shaveh prutah*, nevertheless it is forbidden even if no legal action follows.

"It is forbidden to steal even the smallest quantity—this is the law of the Torah. Anyone who steals whether from a Jew or from a non-Jew even the value of a *prutah* transgresses 'You shall not steal'" (*Choshen Mishpat,* sec. 348, subsec. 1; see Bach on the *Tur,* same sec.). The *Beit Yoseph* adds that the law of less than a *shaveh prutah* in money is equivalent to the law of half a quantity in ritual matters, which is forbidden even if not punishable.

"If one steals even a *shaveh prutah* from his neighbor, it is as though he takes his soul from him" (*Talmud Bavli*, *Bava Kamma* 119a).

In our modern society it has become relatively easy for people to rationalize their fraud in view of the supposedly marginal value of the theft. But all instances of a person's illegally causing loss to his fellow is included in halakhic theft. Such losses include illegally using an employer's telephone or motor car for private purposes, fraudulently reusing postage stamps, benefiting from broken vending machines or telephones, and obtaining illegal benefits from Social Security.

"In general if one is hired for any kind of work, all of his hours are sold to his employer. Any use of these hours by the worker for his personal benefit in any way whatsoever is gross theft" (*Mesillat Yesharim*, chap. 9).

When Rabbi Shimon Skop gave the yeshiva official in Grodna personal letters together with official ones to mail, he was careful to tell him to deduct the amount of his personal postage from his salary.

The Chafetz Chaim once went over to a person in the bathhouse who was using an article that belonged to someone else. He whispered, "A person who washes himself with something that does not belong to him ends up dirtier than before he started" (*Tnuat HaMussar*, vol. 4, p. 120).

Even legal actions that may look fraudulent or that encourage others to steal have to be avoided.

The *Shulchan Arukh* forbids stealing even as a joke or an act meant to annoy the owner. So a minor child who steals is to be punished even though he is not halakhically liable; this instance is distinct, for example, from that of eating nonkosher food, for which he is similarly not liable, yet no punishment is mandatory (*Choshen Mishpat, Hilkhot Geneivah*, sec. 348, subsec. 1).

"Do not enter the property of your fellow to take what is legally yours without permission, so that you will not look like a thief" (*Shulchan Arukh of Baal HaTanya, Hilkhot Gezeilah* 1, *Geneivah*, sec. 26–29, based on *Talmud Bavli, Bava Kamma* 27b).

When one buys stolen goods or goods on which import duty was not paid or when one buys from somebody who does not pay the relevant taxes, the buyer is assisting the seller to steal. "It is not the mouse that steals but the hole" (*Talmud Bavli, Gittin* 45a). One is not allowed to buy goods from those in a position to steal (shepherds operating for others in the *Mishnah*) or from a known thief or anyone who asks to conceal the goods (*Shulchan Arukh, Hilkhot Geneivah*, sec. 458, subsec. 1–5). The Rambam classifies such deeds as aiding somebody to do something forbidden, since if nobody would buy the goods, the thief would not steal them. This is a case of *lifnei iver*—a stumbling block in the path of the blind.

POSTSCRIPT

"All money that is not yours is theft" (Rabbi Yisrael Salanter).

"He who is ready to steal is ready and able to commit every offense. He who cares not to prevent the waste of another's property is equivalent to a thief [by passing on information regarding a hostile takeover or inferior work or a past case of immoral behavior by one of the parties to a transaction]. He who accepts a share in stolen goods will be discovered. A city [or a community] where thieves abound is sure to possess judges who are bribed and police who are corrupt" (Nachman of Bratzlav, *Sefer Hamidot* 62).

When they came to Menachem Mendel of Kotsk to tell him that they thought something had been stolen, the rebbe roared, "It said at Sinai 'Thou shall not steal.'"

6

בְּדַעַת וּבְמִרְמָה

B'DAAT U'V'MIRMA—KNOWINGLY AND DECEITFULLY

Jewish Law forbids the defrauding, deceiving or misleading of people in all matters referring to buying and selling. This law applies equally to Jews and gentiles. "I have seen many people trying to build their wealth on defrauding gentiles but they have not succeeded. Others have dealt scrupulously with all men and God has succeeded their ways" (*Be'er HaGolah, Choshen Mishpat, Hilkhot Geneivah*, sec. 348, subsec. 2).

Theoretically, all parties to a transaction are considered to be equally well informed and fully knowledgeable about all the defects and risks. If one party does not fully disclose or even conceals such defects, the other parties are expected to make the effort to find out all the facts relevant to the transaction. In real life, however, one party, usually the seller of goods or services, has superior knowledge regarding the true price, quality, and quantity of the goods or services. It is often relatively easy to conceal or distort such knowledge, thereby causing loss and damage to the other party. There is a further dimension to the moral problem of nondisclosure. It is often possible to harm others in business simply by creating a false impression and falsifying the details of the transaction without in any way withholding information. This in effect is a secret crime known only to the perpetrator.

B'daat U'v'mirma thus concerns misrepresentation, nondisclosure, and *geneivat daat*, the subtle misleading of people. All three are expressly forbidden by the Torah, which rejects the concept of "Let the buyer beware." Even the lack of a warranty is irrelevant and is considered a "scribe's error" (*Talmud Bavli, Bava Metziah* 49b). Concealing defects in goods or services sold, the lack of full disclosure, and *geneivat daat* become sins to be confessed on Yom Kippur. In the modern economy in which we live, *b'daat u'v'mirma* extends beyond business activities between individuals or corporations to include the documentation and reporting required by government, by regulatory authorities such as the Securities and Exchange Commission, and by the tax authorities. The concept requires careful and constant examination of the gamut of business—advertising, pricing, job seeking, tendering, and financial reporting. The very breadth of activities intrinsic to the merchandising process makes it relatively easy to lose sight of potential fraud. The difficulty of making a clear demarcation between legitimate marketing practices and those that defraud contributes to the blurring of the border between permissible and halakhically forbidden business practices. It becomes easy for the defrauder to legitimize actions against people of other religions or social or ethnic groups that would be unthinkable within his own social unit. Ultimately this defrauding becomes a way of life permitting unethical acts against everyone.

Fraud

"And if you sell anything to your fellowman, or buy anything from the hand of your fellowman, you shall not wrong one another" (Leviticus 25:14).

"Our Sages of blessed memory have said (*Chullin* 94a) that it is also forbidden to fool a non-Jew. It is written, 'The remnant of Israel will do no iniquity and they will not speak falsehood, and a deceiving tongue will not be found in their mouths.' Our Sages have said, 'It is forbidden to paint old vessels to give them the appearance of new ones. It is forbidden to mix the fruits of one field with those of another, though the latter be just as fresh as the first, and though they be worth a dinar and a tresis per measure, and the combination be sold only for a dinar per measure.' [Even though in this case the buyer is actually benefiting, the seller has misrepresented the goods; he himself suffers a religious loss.] If we ask ourselves How is it possible not to attempt to favorably incline the prospective buyer toward the object to be sold and its worth? We must know the great distinction to be made. The efforts made to show the purchaser the true worth and beauty of the object are fitting and proper, but whatever is done to conceal the object's imperfections constitutes deceit and is forbidden. This is an elemental principle in business honesty" (*Mesillat Yesharim*, p. 120 to 121).

"It is forbidden to cheat people [a term used in *halakhah* to include Jews and non-Jews. The Rambam specifically mentions here Jews and gentiles] in business transactions, and to defraud them [literally, 'to steal their minds'—*geneivat daat*]. So if there is a flaw in the article being sold [this would seem to include a substantive defect in information being sold] one is required to declare it to the buyer" (*Shulchan Arukh, Choshen Mishpat*, sec. 228, subsec. 6).

This halakhic obligation of fully disclosing all possible flaws is placed on the seller, who in real life usually has the better information. In those cases, however, such as in the antique trade where the expert buyer usually has better knowledge, the *Shulchan Arukh* would seem to obligate him to disclose the flaws. When the defect is disguised or even not disclosed, the defrauded can claim *mekach ta'ut*. This is usually translated as a "fraudulent sale," but *halakhah* does not require intent to defraud for the sale to become invalid. Furthermore, the injured party is under no obligation to accept the defective goods in return for a discount offered to him. The above source continues to describe fully the remedy offered by *halakhah* for *geneivat daat*.

"If one sells his fellow by weight or by measure or by number and errs even slightly [differentiated from stealing or robbery which require a value, *shaveh prutah*, for litigation], the transaction may be canceled without any limitation of time. [It is interesting to note that violations of the laws of *kashrut*, food ritually pure for Jews to eat, require some minimum quantity, whereas the eating or possession of leavened bread on Passover is transgressed by any amount.] This is different from *onaah* [price gouging], since that applies only to price fraud [and requires *shaveh prutah* and the time required to get expert valuation of the article]. One who sells real estate, slaves, cattle, or movable goods and [the buyer] finds a defect in them which he was not aware of at the time of the sale, the buyer may return it even after many years since this is a *mekach ta'ut*" (*Choshen Mishpat*, sec. 232, subsec. 1–3).

Rabbi Yisrael Salanter, founder of the *Mussar* (Pietist) movement in the Eastern European *yeshivot* of the nineteenth century, taught that just as one checks carefully for blood spots in his eggs [which render them unkosher] so too he should check to see if the money is earned in a kosher manner (*Chafetz Chaim, Sfat Tamim*, chap. 5).

Already some 2,000 years ago, the *Mishnah*, the first codification of the Oral Law, taught (and this was stated in all the Codes), "One may not mix inferior fruit with quality fruit [in order to sell it as first grade]. One may not mix fruit of different orchards [presumably of different qualities] or newly ripened fruit with older fruit [considered to be superior in quality] even if the latter one is more expensive since the buyer wishes to age [or dry them himself and the mixture defrauds him]" (*Choshen Mishpat*, sec. 228, subsec. 1–3; *Mishnah Bava Metziah*, chap. 4, *mishnah* 11).

The same source in subsection nine describes actions that are very prevalent in modern selling of goods and services yet that constitute *geneivat daat* and result in *mekach ta'ut*: "It is forbidden to beautify the man [slave] or animal or utensils: for example to dye the beard of a slave so that he appears younger, or to give bran water to animals since this causes them to appear fat by firming the hair . . . nor is it permissible to paint old utensils so as to hide their blemishes."

The simple examples used in our sources should not blind us to their modern equivalents in present-day marketing and advertising. Selling a used car without revealing that it has been previously involved in a serious accident, even when the damage has been repaired, seems like the *geneivat daat* of the *Shulchan Arukh*. Students obtaining grades or certificates based on material copied from other students or from hidden sources are defrauding potential employers, as does a curriculum vitae that fails to report dismissal from previous employment. Window dressing financial statements to hide corporation's defects is simply a present-day repetition of the cow and utensils incident of the *Mishnah*. Changes in calculating inventory, shifting income or expense from one period to another, and alternative methods of calculating the depreciation of fixed assets will all change a company's profit picture, creating a false impression. The Hebrew term for "window dressing"—*l'yapot* (to make the balance sheet beautiful)—makes this *geneivat daat* clearer than the English version.

It is common practice today to register corporations offshore or in tax havens, primarily to legally evade taxes in the home country, but also to hide the identity of the major shareholders. The same effect is achieved through establishing straw corporations or interlocking companies. These, like corporations, listed or not, which do not make full disclosure in their financial reports, can easily be guilty of *geneivat daat,* since the trading conditions under which they operate are not what they are made out to be. Furthermore, they often enable movement of funds from one unit to another without the knowledge of external parties. The lack of full disclosure becomes a *pgam*, a defect that can damage the interests of shareholders, workers, creditors, and government agencies.

Rabbi Eliyah Chaim Meisel, rabbi of Lodz, called a meeting of the owners of the dairies in his city to discuss a serious halakhic problem. "Regarding the mixing of milk and meat, everything depends on the purity of the milk—if it is heavily diluted I may be able to find a leniency." Without hesitation all the dairies admitted that they heavily diluted their milk. "This is simple deception of your customers," came the unexpected reply of Rabbi Meisel. "If I catch any of you mixing water into your milk again, I will place a public ban on your milk" (*Yechidei Segulah*, p. 125).

"The buyer [negotiating a transaction] should not say these goods are inferior, these goods are worthless [in order to drive down their price]" (*Sefer Chasidim*, sec. 925).

"A person should conduct his affairs in such a way that all who deal with him will know that his original price offer is also his last one" (*Orchot Tzaddikim; Sfat Tamim*, chap. 2).

"It is halakhically permissible to slightly praise the offered goods or services, but it is an act of theft to exaggerate or distort their qualities" (*Arukh HaShulchan, Orach Chaim*, sec. 156, subsec. 3).

A *chasid* of Menachem Mendel of Kotsk was ashamed to appear before his master because of his practice of adulterating the honey he was selling. After a long absence he came and confessed his sin. The rebbe, based on the concept that *asei tov* ("performing good") enables one to depart from evil (*sur merah*), said: "Promise me that you will sell your honey only at a markup of 7 percent rather than the present rate of 6 percent." (This would force him to improve the honey content.)

The *chasid* agreed and subsequently returned. Now the markup was raised to 10 percent. After the next visit, the markup, and therefore the purity, of the honey increased. This continued until at last the dealer was selling pure, unadulterated honey.

Geneivat Daat—Misleading People

There is a wide range of actions and words for creating a false impression about goods or services. This misdeed is distinct from the fraud perpetrated through disguising defects or failing to reveal them. Much advertising is knowingly geared to create a false impression in order to sell the goods or services, even though the goods are not flawed in any way.

The ruling of the *Shulchan Arukh* regarding *geneivat daat* is a simple yet effective description of how such false impressions are used in marketing. "It is forbidden to sell the meat of an animal which died [of natural causes] as though it were slaughtered ritually [kosher] even to an idolater [who halakhically is not bound to eat kosher meat]" (*Choshen Mishpat*, sec. 228, subsec. 6). Even though no damage spiritual or physical was caused to the idolater, nevertheless, the seller created a false impression leading the gentile to think that he, the seller, was doing him a special favor selling him meat fit for Jews. Is the advertising of "last day of sale" when in fact it was the only day of the sale not exactly this? So too the slashing of prices, which were only just raised, in order to create the impression that the buyer was getting a bargain? It may be *geneivat daat* when goods are wrapped or packaged in such a way as to look bigger or contain more items. During periods of price control, firms may use the old containers to sell less content at the old price; the lesser weight may be marked, but the intent to deceive is clear.

"It is not permitted to tell a customer 'Somebody has already paid me this amount for this item [or] I bought it cheaply, so that you can now sell it for more.' About this the prophet Zephania says 'The remnant of Israel shall not do evil nor speak falsehoods; neither shall a deceitful tongue be found in their mouth' (3:13). Rather he should behave in the simplicity—*temimut*—of a righteous person and should say in faith—*bitachon*—'This is how much I am charging for it, irrespective of what I paid for it'" (*Sefer Ya'atzu Chasidim*, p. 163). The same source continues: "A person should not say to a potential customer, 'I bought it for such and such a sum,' or 'People have already made a down payment,' when it is untrue. This is like the salesmen who are girded in lies and deceit. . . . Why should you lie? Fix a price and say 'Below this I will not sell' . . . and the lips of truth are established forever" (p. 193).

"A purchaser should not say, 'This is a bad deal at a high price.' Rather he should say, 'This is what I want to pay you'" (*Sefer Chasidim*, 925).

"*Lo tonu*—'You shall not oppress'; this refers to one who steals someone's eye—that is, one who makes something good on the outside when it is bad on the inside" (*Sforno*, Leviticus 25:17).

Halakhah does not require that the misleading information or defects in the goods or services be deliberate or even made with the perpetrator's knowledge. It is sufficient that a flaw exists and the buyer or seller suffers. In the modern sophisticated market, agents, consultants, corporate directors, accountants, lawyers, and bankers provide information such as market trends, evaluations, and viability of investments. It is pertinent therefore to bear the following references in mind.

"Whoever tells a person to lend money to another because he is trusted and it turns out not to be so, he is liable to make restitution" (Rama, *Shulchan Arukh, Choshen Mishpat*, sec. 129, subsec. 2).

"*A priori* one may not give another faulty information, knowingly or deceitfully. So liability for such information arises not only when some actual act [sale of goods] is done but also when a mere statement is made. For example, a coin was shown to a moneychanger to verify, and he validated it. Later the coin was found to be counterfeit or nonlegal tender. Now if payment was paid for the expert opinion, the moneychanger [the consultant] is liable to make restitution. Even if no payment was made, the moneychanger would be liable if he was not really an expert [inexperienced or still in training professionally]. Only where he is a recognized authority is he exempt from making restitution, if he received no payment for his services" (*Arukh HaShulchan, Choshen Mishpat*, sec. 306, subsec. 13).

Ever present in Judaism in all monetary crimes is the moral effect on the perpetrator over and above the legal obligation incurred. The Torah warns us against being a false or unrighteous witness. Such a witness differs from one giving false evidence. Unrighteousness refers to the false nature of the individual's being.

"This is to prevent a rabbinic judge from hearing one party before the arrival of another and to warn the litigants against presenting themselves before the court without the opponent being present" (*Talmud Bavli, Sanhedrin* 7b).

"One says to another, since I only have one witness [Jewish law requires at least two], go and stand next to my witness. You will say nothing nor give evidence, simply stand there [thus creating the false impression that the litigant has the required two witnesses]. This is forbidden as it is written, 'You shall distance yourself from a false matter.'" So too "One may not say I will claim (falsely) that Reuven owes me 200 coins when he only owes 100, in order to panic him into paying the true amount; as it is written 'You shall distance yourself from a false matter'" (*Talmud Bavli, Shavuot* 31a, commenting on Exodus 23:7).

The story of Rabbi Safra teaches how one should refuse to benefit from creating a false impression, even by otherwise legitimate actions. "Rabbi Safra was standing in prayer when a buyer approached him to purchase his goods. When the buyer received no reaction to his original offer, he raised the price, taking the rabbi's silence for rejection. As the prayer continued, so the bidding rose until finally Rabbi Safra showed that he had finished. Hastily the merchant counted out the coins of his last offer, only to find that Rabbi Safra returned to him the difference between that and his first offer" (*Rashi, Talmud Bavli, Makkot 24a,* and *Bava Basra* 88a*)*.

This story forms the basis of a *teshuvah* about a storekeeper in modern New York who wished to raise his prices but had forgotten to change the price tags that gave a lower price. The rabbi ruled that he was required to sell the goods according to the price tag (*Beit Avi*, pt. 4, sec. 185).

Theft of Intellectual Property—Copyrights, Tapes, Cassettes

One of today's most complicated moral issues revolves around the ownership of intellectual property. The modern explosion in the communications industry, the high-tech nature of storing and transmitting information, and the constant innovation have created what is probably the newest moral issue in business. Of major ethical concern is the use of the information communicated by companies or individuals other than the inventors, creators, or sources of the information. Not at issue are the legal halakhic questions of whether such use necessitates payments for loss of income or whether compensation must be made for infringing copyright or whether the public good justifies protecting intellectual property. The question is whether such actions are permitted, not whether the perpetrators are liable.

"One whose eyes are attracted to evil saying 'what's yours is mine' is an evil person . . . concerning whom Jeremiah prophesied, 'This is the word of God regarding one who steals the words of his fellowman [like Chananiah ben Azur, who repeated the words of Jeremiah as though they were his own]'" (*Teshuvah Mei Ahavah*, pt. 3).

"One who repeats something [knowledge] in the name of its source brings redemption to the world" (*Mishnah Avot,* chap. 6, *mishnah* 6; also *Talmud Bavli*, *Megillah* 15a).

Conversely, "One who repeats something without revealing its source is referred to by the verse 'You shall not rob the poor for they are poor'" (Proverbs 22:22; *Midrash Tanchuma;* Numbers 22).

"A person should not sin after his father's death for the sake of the honor of the departed. This is the case of one who knows that his father did not write the commentary yet commanded him, 'You will write my name as the author of this book so that people will refer to me—may his name be blessed.' The son shall not do so but will publish the book under its true authorship [shall not steal the property of the author] even as it is written in the *Sifre*, [the verse], 'You shall not remove your neighbor's landmark' which the ancients commanded that one may not ascribe the teachings [intellectual property] of Rabbi Eliezer to Rabbi Yehoshua" (*Sefer Chasidim*, sec. 586).

"It is important that one should ascribe information to its source and not steal the mind of the originator since this is worse than stealing money" (*Sh'nai Luchot Habrit, Shavuot* 183b).

"If one clothes himself in the Torah [knowledge] of his fellow and does not reveal the source, he is a thief. This even if in fact the author does not lose anything [which would not be the case if the author lost royalties or sales as a result of piracy] while the thief has a benefit. One is not allowed to have a benefit from another's property without his permission except when the owner does not mind. However, there is nobody who does not value the creations of his mind and does not wish that another, who did not labor for it, should benefit, so this is robbery" (*Teshuvot Machaneh Chaim*, *Choshen Mishpat*, pt. 2, sec. 49; see also *Choshen Mishpat*, sec. 343).

"One who stole a commentary on the Torah and swore an oath that he would not return it until he had copied it was told that there was an opinion that he could do so. However, such a one is a thief and did not even fulfill the obligation of Torah study since it is a *mitzvah* fulfilled fraudulently, *mitzvah haba be'aveirah* (*Teshuvot HaRif*, sec. 133; reproduced in *Teshuvot HaRasbah,* pt. 5, sec. 286).

Because some rabbinic opinion held that intellectual property could not be stolen, the Maharam Shick wrote, "It is forbidden to repeat commentaries without revealing their source, since we are commanded, 'You shall remove yourself from a false matter' or because of *geneivat daat* [even if it is not considered theft halakhically]" (*Teshuvot Maharam Shick; Yoreh De'ah*, sec. 156).

"[Although heirs cannot inherit intangible assets or a benefit that is not considered money, still the heirs can prevent somebody's publishing their father's commentaries.] In this matter we follow the [copyright] law of the land since in all matters where integrity demands it in fulfillment of 'you shall do that which is good and honest,' *dina demalkhuta* applies . . ." (Rabbi Shimon Sofer, in addendum to *Teshuvot Chatam Sofer* , pt. 7, sec. 232).

There is no reason to doubt that the obligation to reveal the source of the information and the injunctions about not reprinting or presenting it as one's original work would apply beyond the Torah commentaries referred to in the above sources and would include tapes, software, books, and so on. Furthermore, their unauthorized reproduction may be forbidden as constituting damage to the author or creator, who suffers a loss of sales or even prestige. When damage is indirect or far removed in time or space, the perpetrator may not be liable for compensation. Yet such damage is forbidden.

POSTSCRIPT

The most insidious deception is self-deception, which helps create gray areas of conduct where in fact no such areas exist in *halakhah*.

Commenting on the verse "thou shall not steal" (Leviticus 19:11), Menachem Mendel of Kotsk said "not only is it forbidden to steal from others, but also one should not steal your own consciousness. One should not deceive oneself."

"Rav Huna said, 'When a person sins once and then repeats the sin, it becomes permitted to him.' Did he really mean permitted to him? No [he meant that] it becomes to him as though it is permitted" (*Talmud Bavli*, *Kiddushin* 40a).

7

בְּהוֹנָאַת רֵעַ

B'honaat Reah—By Oppressing a Fellowman

Oppression is not only blatantly physical. There is also monetary oppression, which occurs whenever one exploits others' ignorance of market conditions or their physical, psychological, or financial distress. Monetary oppression includes overcharging or excessive profits and withholding wages or payments due (*onaat mamon*). There is also psychological oppression, which occurs when one does comparative shopping without any intent to purchase or embarrasses employees or competitors in public. Although these references are to the business arena, they apply equally to public officials, who often wield more power to oppress than do ordinary businesspeople.

***Onaat Mamon*—Price Gouging**

"And you shall not grieve one another and you shall fear your God for I, God, am your God. Carry out My statutes and observe and carry out My social ordinances. Then you will be sustained by the Land in security" (Leviticus 25:14–17).

"[This verse is part of the laws of *Yovel*, the Jubilee Year.] *Shmittah* and *Yovel* introduce the concept of God into all the business transactions of man, and make it clear that all men live and work together on the one soil of God, in the one Land of God, where God is the Master and Owner of all property and where, exercising His rights of ownership, He expects us to pay Him homage in all our transactions. The obvious corollary to this idea, i.e., that all of communal life takes place before the eye of God, is that God is present not only in the Temple but also in the midst of all business and commerce transacted by the members of the nation. He will support and bless these transactions in His Land and upon His soil, and all the individuals involved in them only if they bring happiness and prosperity to all; if no one 'grieves' the other; if no one abuses the position he has attained on God's soil, or the breath he draws in God's Land, to cheat or 'grieve' another; and if that one basic truth of all truths, 'I am God, your God,' with all its consequences, becomes permanently imbedded in every phase of our lives, both as individuals and as a nation" (S. R. Hirsch on Leviticus 25:17).

These verses from Leviticus imply that the protection of *onaah* is provided for those suffering from overcharging. Any sale above one-sixth of the market price, which obviously includes profit, may be canceled by a rabbinic court. A sale less than one-sixth is waived from consideration; most people do not protest against slight variations in the price. The primary issue is not one of price fraud, as *onaah* is usually translated, but of oppression. The seller or buyer operating below or above the market price is seen as oppressing the other party by exploiting the lack of knowledge. This idea of oppression is borne out by the use of the same Hebrew word here as in the case of the widow and orphan where no element of price fraud exists, as in Exodus 22:22. It is also amply shown by this ruling:

"He who buys and sells in good faith cannot be guilty of *onaah*. If the seller says to the purchaser, 'This article which I am selling for 200 is sold in the market for 100' there is no case of *onaah*. [He may include in his selling price the costs of transportation, porterage, and hotel expenses but not his own wages as a laborer. Now if he publicly declares his profit margin, there is no claim of *onaah*]" (*Mishneh Torah*, *Hilkhot Mechirah* 13:4).

Even when the injured party has full knowledge and agrees to the price, the rabbis uphold his right to the protection of the just price in those cases where he has been coerced.

"The buyer agreed that he had known that he was being overcharged and nevertheless agreed to the sale. However, he had just obtained a large order for goods from a major customer. In order to satisfy this order, he urgently required the raw material so had no option to pay the exaggerated price [charged by his supplier who knew of his need]. This is similar to the ferryman case in *Bava Kamma* 115a, where the fugitive agreed to pay far more than the usual price since he was being pursued. In accordance with the Sages, I rule that Reuven is entitled to repayment of the difference between the price charged and the market price" (*Teshuvat Bayit Chadash*, sec. 65; see also Rama, *Choshen Mishpat*, sec. 227, subsec. 7).

"Just as the buyer has protection of *onaah*, so too does the seller" (*Shulchan Arukh*, *Choshen Mishpat*, sec. 227).

The question of *onaah* arises even in the case of economic activities conducted by educational institutions and charitable organizations. Many authorities do not hold that these organizations have the same status as the Temple property (*hekdesh*), the transactions of which were exempt from *onaah*. Alternatively, "The laws of *onaah* apply to books sold by the library when it sold excess copies of books at a price above market price. The yeshiva students rightfully assumed that the books were being sold at below market price. This is not the same as those charitable auctions where people go prepared to pay much more simply because of the cause behind it" (*Mishneh Halakhot*, vol. 9, sec. 364).

The *halakhah* sets a cut-off point of one-sixth, which does not apply to real estate and promissory notes. The courts give no redress for amounts less than a *shaveh prutah*; nevertheless, overcharging is forbidden even in these cases; all that is referred to, is the legal compensation of the injured party.

"The main admonition, however, applies both to land and movable property: for we were warned not to defraud people deliberately. But the difference between them is that if the overcharging on movable goods was found to amount to more than a sixth, the sale is nullified. For it is the way of people not to tolerate price gouging beyond that with movable goods. With land, though, since land is something that endures forever, it is the way of people to forgive any price gouging after they have purchased it. Now, the proof of these words that the prohibition against *onaah* applies with land too, is that here [in Leviticus] it is principally about landed property that this admonition is written.

"The root reason for the precept is evident for it is something to which the intelligence attests. Had it not been written, justice would have required it to be written. For it is not right to acquire people's property by way of lying and deceit. Rather, everyone should attain by his toil that which God has graciously bestowed on him, in truth and honesty. For each and every one there will be gainful benefit in this condition: for just as one will not wrong others, others will equally not wrong him. Consequently, matters turn out equally well for all, and it is of great benefit in the civilizing of the world, which the Eternal Lord, blessed is He, formed to be settled" (*Sefer HaChinukh*, *mitzvah* 337).

"Humans' desire and pursuit of worldly physical pleasure causes them to oppress their fellows in all their business dealings, their buying and selling, and their trade. To rule out the possibility that people would think that since this oppression is not actual theft or robbery it is not forbidden, our Torah warns us about it by saying 'Do not oppress each other.' This is to teach us that a person is obligated to act faithfully in his business dealings, and not to desire to overcharge for what he sells or to underpay for what he buys. Despite the fact that people are only in business to profit, nonetheless the Torah commands us not to buy or sell an item for more or less than a sixth of its value. The reason is that a sixth is a small amount, which, the Sages explained, a person would forgive when he trades. However, even though they [the Sages] declared that at this amount a person forgives [the over- or underpayment] and that a court does not enforce the annulment of a sale or the return of the overcharge, nevertheless somebody who wants to walk in the paths of piety will sell goods for their actual value" (*Menorat HaMaor*, *Ner* 1, *Klal* 2, *Chelek* 2, chap. 5).

Onaat Devarim

Employers, senior executives, managers, and others in authority can all harass, embarrass, or exploit other people. It is in their power to inflict economic loss on employees through dismissal, transfer to less desirable locations or jobs, and on suppliers through using other suppliers. Price exploitation affects only the material welfare of others, but verbal exploitation that comes from the hidden, secret recesses of the perpetrator's mind affects their very souls.

The repetition of the law of *onaah* in Leviticus 25:17 is concluded by "I am the Lord," which expresses Divine displeasure and intervention for *onaat devarim*.

"Rabbi Chisda said: 'All the gates [of Heaven] are locked except for the gates of [the prayers of those who suffer from] *onaah*. . . .' Rabbi Elazar said: 'Everything is punished by the hand of a messenger except for *onaah* [caused, which is punished directly by God]. . . .' Rabbi Abbahu said: 'There are three sins before which the curtain [of Divine knowledge] is not closed: *onaah*, robbery, and idolatry'" (*Talmud Bavli*, *Bava Metziah* 59a).

"And the person who does this [verbal oppression] will receive a strong punishment by the Holy One Himself. The principle is: everything that causes distress to another person with words is oppression through words. In order to know which things upset one's fellow, one should always observe the words of the rabbis, 'What is hateful to you do not do to your fellow.' According to the seriousness of this [sin] a person has to be extremely watchful, because a person is liable to care about and be sensitive about, and to get upset about even the smallest comments that people make to him . . ." (*Pele Yoetz*, *Onaah*).

"And you shall not grieve (*lo tonu*), this is the rich purchaser who buys from the poor seller and he should remember that 'I am the Lord who makes low and raises up'" (Abarbanel).

Simple versions of *onaah* are the large corporations who delay payment to small firms, or smaller firms who have only one major purchaser who is able to shave the firm's profits to a minimum or reduce them to bankruptcy in times of recession.

Emek Davar on Leviticus 25:17 comments, "The Torah places this prohibition next to business dealings because in these activities a person is most likely to be affected but the law applies to all activities."

"Just as there is wrongdoing in business [price gouging] so too there is the same oppression in words. A person should not inquire, 'How much does this cost,' when one has no intention of buying [or is simply doing comparative shopping]. [This would seem to apply only to those businesses that do not factor browsing, comparative shopping, or impulse buying into their cost analysis because the others suffer no psychological damage.] If ass drivers are looking for a source for fodder [this would apply to anybody searching for a supplier], one may not say to them, 'Go to so and so who has such goods' when one knows that he neither has them nor ever sold them. Rabbi Yehudah says one may not even look at the goods [for sale] if one does not have the money [to buy them. The *Meiri* comments that the seller suffers mentally but also wastes time showing the articles since he thinks he is going to make a sale]" (*Talmud Bavli*, *Bava Metziah* 48b).

Employer–Employee Relations

This is an area in which the power to harass, embarrass, and inflict psychological damage is almost unlimited and calls for constant awareness and moral restraint on the part of employers or managers. Sexual harassment, so prevalent and so easily facilitated by employer–employee relationships, is specially abhorrent: it combines all the elements of oppression with the sexual immorality forbidden by Judaism.

"Over your brethren the Children of Israel, one over the other you shall not rule overbearingly" (Leviticus 25:46).

"A person must not subjugate his fellowman. If others fear him [whether for political, social, or economic reasons] or are embarrassed to challenge his opinion [often a cause of superior–dependent friction], he should not command them to do even a minor task unless it is in accordance with their will and for their benefit" (Rabbenu Yona, *Shaarei Teshuvah* 3:60).

Often employees and subordinates are embarrassed by their superiors' or employers' very presence, which easily becomes a method of oppression. "If someone who is clever and trained in logical argument [usually applicable to employers or people in managerial authority] goes to listen to a local rabbi who is modest, not clever, nor trained in logical argument [equally applicable to the less trained, less experienced employees who are more dependent on their superiors] who becomes embarrassed by the person merely sitting there . . . then the clever person has sinned even though he did not even ask any difficult questions" (*Sefer Chasidim* 972).

"Just as there is oppression with words, so too there is oppression with a biased or angry eye, whereby a person looks unpleasantly at someone else" (*Sefer Yeraim*, *Siman* 51).

Employees stand in relationship to their superiors in exactly the same social and psychological status as the widow and orphan. Defenseless against abuse, ignorant of their rights and powerless to defend them, and constantly made aware of their economic dependency on others, they are easily abused. So we should bear in mind, "You shall not afflict any widow or orphan. If you oppress them and they cry out to Me, I will surely hear their cry and My anger shall be inflamed" (Exodus 22:20–23).

All too often those in authority taunt those subject to them by asking for their opinion even though they know full well that the employees neither know the answer nor are able to express themselves properly. This *halakhah* of Maimonides clearly provides needed guidance. "If a question is asked about some branch of knowledge, one should not say to someone who does not know that field, 'What would you answer to that?' or 'What do you think about that?'" (*Mishneh Torah*, *Hilkhot Mechirah*, chap. 14, *halakhah* 14).

"We excommunicate the person who embarrasses his fellow with words, until he appeases the one whom he embarrassed, to an extent commensurate with the injured person's honor" (Rav Shira Gaon as quoted by the Rosh in *Perek HaGozel* and the *Beit Yosef*, *Choshen Mishpat*, sec. 420).

"And the Egyptians made the Children of Israel serve with labor that exhausts the human body—*befarekh* . . ." (Exodus 1:13). "The severity did not lie in the actual physical labor, normal in many occupations; . . . rather the aim was to oppress us with cunning . . . presented as mild and harmless. . . . They forbade us our day of rest [needed both for spiritual growth and physical renewal]. . . . The labor was exhausting because in determining the work a person was to do, no account was taken of their suitability—circumstances, aptitude, capability, and bodily strength. On the contrary, they took pains to select the jobs for which the person was least suitable. In *Talmud Bavli*, *Sotah* 11, Rabbi Shmuel ben Nachmani taught that 'men were given work usually preformed by women and vice versa'" (Rabbi Dr. Marcus Lehman, *commentary on the Haggadah of Pesach*, pp. 114–115).

Other commentators have described the oppression as simply being given useless or unnecessary jobs simply to fill the time of the worker. In this way, any dignity flowing from the satisfaction of a job well done or from any creativity associated with the work was destroyed.

Withholding Payment

"There are actions which desecrate God's Name when they are done by one who is considered to be a Torah scholar or known as a righteous person, even though when done by ordinary people they may perhaps not be considered as sins. For example, when one buys goods but does not pay promptly [at the arranged due date. In this way he causes his creditors loss and anxiety since they have to badger him and repeatedly claim their debts]" (*Mishneh Torah*, *Hilkhot Yesodei HaTorah*, chap. 5, *halakhah* 11).

"Rabbi Chaim Medina, the author of the halakhic encyclopedia *Sde Hemed*, once gave a shoemaker who delivered goods to his home a large note. The shoemaker, not having change, offered to come back again another day to collect his debt. 'Why should you lose time or money because it's too late for me to go to someone's house to get change? I have an obligation to pay you immediately,' said the rabbi. He therefore borrowed the money from a neighbor to pay the shoemaker" (*Yechidei Segulah*, p. 83).

"What is an example of *chillul Hashem*? Rav said, 'If I took meat from the butcher and delayed payment [he would say I'm a thief and would learn to treat theft lightly—Rashi]. . . . When Abbaya bought meat from two partners, he would pay both of them [the full amount. This was in case one of the partners did not know that the other had been paid and there would be desecration of God's Name—Rashi] and then he would get them together to get back the amount owed to him'" (*Talmud Bavli*, *Yoma* 86a).

"It is forbidden for a debtor to withhold payment, saying to the creditor, 'Tomorrow I'll pay you,' and then tomorrow not pay him if he, the debtor, has the money" (*Shulchan Arukh*, *Choshen Misphat*, sec. 97, subsec. 3).

Postscript

"Reb Shraga Frank [father-in-law of Rabbi Isser Zalman Meltzer, Chief Rabbi of Jerusalem, and Rabbi Moshe Mordechai Epstein, the author of the halakhic code *Arukh HaShulchan*] was once entertaining a group of very prominent people. He rang a bell for the maid to come and serve the tea but she did not come. Even though he rang a few times, there was still no answer. One of the guests remarked that perhaps if he were stricter he would get better service. 'This gives me happiness,' said Reb Shraga with a smile. 'I'm always worried that I have become overbearing or oppressing and thereby violating a Torah prohibition. When I see she does not fear me, this reassures me that I am indeed not doing so'" (*T'nuat HaMussar*, vol. 3, fn. 6, p. 40).

"What is brigandage—*oshek*? When one extends a loan [or credit] or is employed by somebody and it is not possible to claim the payment since the debtor or the employer is violent and harsh. It is in reference to this that the Torah told us, 'You shall not oppress your fellow' (Leviticus 19:13)" (*Mishneh Torah*, *Hilkhot Gezeilah VeAveidah*, chap. 1, *halakhah* 4).

8

בְּחֹזֶק יָד

B'chozek Yad—By Violence

Violence is usually associated with bodily abuse or other physical actions. Force, however, may also be used in the market and with regard to people's money or property. Withholding by force that which belongs to another or withholding wages due, denying loans that were taken, misusing trust funds or clients' investment monies, abusing charitable funds, squatting in another's home, coercing others by social pressure or by badgering them to make a sale [even at market price]: all these are considered to be forms of violence.

"What is robbery? One who takes the money of another by force, as for example . . . one who trespasses and takes by force an article or a servant or a draught animal [modern machinery] and uses them against the will of the owner, or enters a field and eats of its produce—and all similar acts—this is robbery. What is oppression? This is where money or property of his fellow is given to him willingly [as a loan, or in trust or to invest] but when the owners demand their property back, he refuses to give it back to them. And it is forbidden from the Torah to rob even something of a relatively insignificant value [*kol shehu*]. Even a non-Jew [is included here so that] it is forbidden to rob him or to oppress him" (*Mishneh Torah*, *Hilkhot Gezeilah VeAveidah*, chap. 1, *halakhot* 2–4).

Even a momentary taking possession of another's property without their knowledge is considered robbery (*Shulchan Arukh*, *Choshen Mispat*, sec. 359, subsec. 5).

So too certain forms of betting, gambling, and speculation in business where the other party only agrees hypothetically but actually depended on the opposite happening is a form of robbery (*Shulchan Arukh*, *Chosen Mishpat*, secs. 207 and 370).

Withholding Wages

"You shall not keep overnight [delay] the wages of a day laborer" (Leviticus 19:13), and "You shall not oppress a day laborer who is poor and in need, whether of your brethren or of the strangers that are in your land—on his day you shall give him his wage and let not the sun go down on it, for he is poor and sets his heart upon it. Let him not cry out to God against you and it would be a sin upon you" (Deuteronomy 24:14–15).

The repetition in Deuteronomy is used by the *Sifri* to teach that even though one is obligated to punctual payment irrespective of the economic situation of the employee, withholding wages is even more heinous before God in the case of the poor. This teaching applies to non-Jews who renounce idolatry and accept the Seven Noachide laws. The *Sifri* continues with an accurate insight into the psychology of the worker by explaining that he "sets his heart upon it" and "for the wages he even risks his life, undertaking dangerous work, ascends scaffolding, and so on, so that one who withholds wages, it is as though he took the very life of the employee." Even the financial life of the employee is at risk. Delayed payment forces the employee to depend on expensive consumer credit or to become entrapped in an unbreakable cycle of usurious loans.

For the employer, withholding wages represents an interest-free loan, a nontaxable windfall, with a financial profit to be earned. Indeed in almost all countries, unorganized labor, migrant workers, illegal aliens, part-time workers, and other powerless groups are regularly exposed to such exploitation. The Sages readily understood this when they interpreted the "sets his life upon it" in Deuteronomy as referring to the employer's lust.

"One who withholds payment of wages transgresses four negative commandments and violates one positive one. . . . You shall not oppress, you shall not rob, you shall not keep overnight (Leviticus 19:13), you shall not allow the sun to set on it [the wages] (Deuteronomy 24:16) and you will surely give him his wage on its appointed time (Deuteronomy, *ibid.)" (Mishneh Torah, Hilkhot S'khirut,* chap. 11, *halakhot* 1–2).

"This does not only apply to a worker hired for a given number of hours. Even if you hire a worker to do a small job or a service of minimal value . . . all the laws of prompt payment apply. A worker employed for a week, for a month, for a year, or even for seven years: as soon as he finishes the job he must be paid that same day before the sun sets or if he finishes the job at night, he must be paid by daybreak. All of these apply both to the wages of a person and to the rental for any asset . . . [subcontracting and mechanical equipment—*Mishneh Torah*]. [Land seems to be a halakhic issue] yet the Vilna Gaon and many authorities hold that rent for land and for a house need to be promptly paid [as an application of payment of wages over and above the question of theft]" (*Chafetz Chaim*, *Ahavat Chesed*, chap. 8).

The assumption in the above, regarding the hire of nonhuman resources, is that the provision of such services is done primarily by small units, on whom the disruption of cash flow through delayed or irregular payment would have much the same effect as in the case of an employee.

Loans and Trust Funds

"It is forbidden for a debtor to borrow money and use it carelessly and waste it so that no assets remain for the creditor to collect his debt from [especially relevant to excessive and injudicious use of credit cards and consumer credit]. One who does so is called an evil one" (*Shulchan Arukh*, *Choshen Mishpat*, sec. 97, subsec. 4).

"One may not say to one's neighbor [in respect to a debt] come tomorrow, come tomorrow [thus postponing the payment]" (Proverbs 3:28).

"One who borrows and does not pay is evil and the Righteous One will have mercy and repay" (Psalms 37:21).

"What is an evil way from which people should depart? Rabbi Shimon says, One who borrows and does not repay. It is irrelevant whether he borrows from man or whether he borrows from God. [God Himself Who is Justice personified will pay the creditor when the borrower defaults and then will claim payment from the debtor—God as it were, now becomes the creditor]" (*Ethics of the Fathers*, chap. 2, *mishnah* 9).

"Your neighbor's money should be precious to you, as your own" (*Ethics of the Father*, chap. 2, *mishnah* 12).

"When the creditor claims his debt [in the *bet din*] even though he is rich and the debtor is poor we do not distort justice but will enforce the claim to the end . . . even the special *Shabbat* and festival clothes [of the wife and children, as opposed to their regular weekday needs] can be claimed by the creditor. It is unnecessary to state that rings or jewelry of gold and silver all belong to the creditor. . . . [The courts will] leave the debtor from all his assets including even a needle, food for thirty days, clothing suitable to his status for twelve months, but he should not be allowed to wear [luxury clothes like] silk or cloth embroidered with gold thread. A bed and mattress to sleep on and a chair to sit on and his *tefillin*. . . . His wife and minor children are not included [since the creditor is not obligated to support them]" (*Mishneh Torah*, *Hilkhot Ishut*, chap. 2, *halakhah* 2; *Mishneh Torah*, *Hilkhot Malveh VeLoveh*, chap. 1, *halakhot* 4–7).

These stern yet just *halakhot* can help prevent a common practice under modern bankruptcy laws, especially in the case of a limited liability corporation, where it is possible for a bankrupt debtor to live according to his previous lifestyle at the creditor's expense. The same *halakhah* demands from the creditor both that he not abuse his power and that he be prepared to waive his rights to full payment. This latter, however, is an act of charity and does not contradict the demands of justice.

"A creditor who seizes an article as security for his debt from the hand of the debtor [outside his house], without the instructions of the *bet din*, is a robber, even though the validity of the debt is recognized . . . where the creditor enters the debtor's house [forbidden even to the officers of the court since it infringes on the dignity of the debtor] and takes something as a pledge, he too is a robber" (*Mishneh Torah*, *Hilkhot Gezeilah VeAveidah*, chap. 3, *halakhah* 16).

"It is forbidden to oppress the debtor and to force him to pay his debt when the creditor knows that he has no money or assets to pay him with. . . . It is even forbidden [for the creditor] to show himself to the debtor since this increases his shame, knowing that he is unable to repay the debt" (*Shulchan Arukh, Choshen Mishpat*, sec. 97, subsec. 2).

Lawyers, accountants, and banks often receive money to be held in trust for clients. These funds are meant for retirement, minor children, or people unable to manage their own affairs. Many recent financial scandals have arisen from improper use of pension funds in order to protect the assets of a failing corporation or entrepreneur, and trustees sometimes borrow for personal use from trust funds under their care. Although a trustee intends to replace the money in the future, this promise may not materialize. All these acts are considered robbery as well as failure to perform a fiduciary obligation. Jewish sources, however, provide a different frame of reference for guardians and trustees of other people's money.

"A trustee may not use the entrusted article even if he did not intend to steal it but only to use it [temporarily] even if there is no damage done . . . because he uses it without the owner's knowledge and is therefore a robber" (*Shulchan Arukh, Choshen Mishpat*, sec. 292, subsec. 1).

"People were used to leave money for orphans in trust with the father of Shmuel. When the father died, Shmuel was not with him, and people started to call him 'the son of one who embezzled money' [since the orphans' money had not been found]. Said Shmuel to his father [who appeared to him in the cemetery after prolonged prayer], 'Where is the orphans' money?' 'Go and collect it from under the pole of the millstone. The top and bottom [layers of money] are ours, the middle belongs to the orphans. I did this because I was afraid that the money could be stolen. Then, the lost money [the top layer] would be ours; if the soil would have damaged the money at the bottom, it would have damaged our money'" (*Talmud Bavli*, *Berakhot* 18b).

"The custodians of charitable funds [the most clear-cut example of trust money] may not separate from each other [when collecting the money] unless they remain in sight of each other [in order to avert suspicion that they are stealing by collecting the money separately]. . . . They may not count the charity money five coins at a time but only each coin separately to avert suspicion [that they are taking two but only counting one] as it is written, 'And you shall be clean before God and Israel' [Numbers 32:22]" (*Shulchan Arukh*, *Yoreh De'ah*, sec. 257, subsec. 1).

"In order that trustees should be clean before God and Israel, they should [be accountable and] present valid accounts [even though in theory people are considered righteous and not in need of accounting]. This [assumption] refers to trustees who are considered honest people, but those who appointed themselves by force [or by fraud] are obligated to provide proper accounts of their activities" (Rama on *Choshen Mishpat*, sec. 2).

Coercive Trading

Violence can be expressed through trading methods in which buyer or seller badgers, overwhelms, or pressures people to enter into transactions against their better judgment or against their will. Financial scandals have occurred when brokers bullied clients into buying unnecessary or excessive insurance. Authors, charitable institutions, or direct mail houses may send unsolicited books or other goods to people and place them in the uncomfortable position of paying for them, returning them, or keeping them without paying. Commercial travelers and real estate agents often pressure people to close a deal or order goods without allowing them time or liberty to freely consider the options. In hostile takeovers, shareholders are pestered and overwhelmed by mailings and advertisements geared to get them to agree to the takeover, while those owning sizable blocks of shares are subject to further pressure.

"It is forbidden to force somebody to sell his property even if he pays the market price. He is, however, not disqualified as being a robber from bearing witness [since the goods or articles were finally legally sold by the owner]. However, rabbinic law disqualifies him.

"One who covets his fellow's house, his goods, or anything [belonging to him] which may be purchased and subsequently persuades the owner's friends to influence or persuade him to sell [or to buy despite his unwillingness] transgresses the Divine injunction 'Thou shall not covet' (Exodus 20:14). . . . One who lusts after anything belonging to his neighbor because he thereafter contrives and speculates as to how he can purchase it . . . transgresses the Divine commandment [in the repetition of the Decalogue in Deuteronomy 5:18] 'Thou shall not lust' since lust is something in the heart [as distinct from the coercive action referred to in the previous section]" (*Shulchan Arukh*, *Choshen Mishpat*, sec. 358, subsec. 9–10).

Maimonides applies the injunction against coveting even to those cases where the owner is offered much money, presumably above market price, and actually loses nothing. Throughout the discussion in the Codes, it is the spiritual basis of covetousness and lusting after other people's possessions that is the issue, not the financial or material damage, if any, suffered.

Aiding and Abetting

In all the variations of the *b'chozek yad* or "violence," as described above, the role of those who benefit indirectly from the forbidden actions, yet are not directly involved, is never forgotten.

"It is forbidden to buy from a thief [or a robber (*Hilkhot Gezeilah*, chap. 5, *halakhah* 1)] any stolen goods. To do so is a great sin since he strengthens the hands of the evildoer [by allowing him to enjoy the profit of his immoral act] and [there is an additional sin since] he causes the thief [or robber] to steal in the future. [After all] if he would not find a customer, he would not steal. Regarding this it is written, 'He who shares with the thief [if he himself does not steal] hates [loses] his soul' (Proverbs 29:24). [Regarding the robber, Maimonides claims that he transgresses. 'You shall not place a stumbling block in the path of the blind' (Leviticus 19:14)]" (*Mishneh Torah*, *Hilkhot Geneivah*, chap. 5, *halakhah* 1).

"It is forbidden to buy anything that is presumed stolen [even if the seller is not the thief]. So too even if only the majority of the goods are stolen it is forbidden to buy. . ." (*Mishneh Torah*, *Hilkhot Geneivah*, chap. 6, *halakhah* 1).

"One may not buy anything from any artisan who sells goods [scrap, remnants, shavings, threads, and so on], which according to the law of the land [or the business custom] does not belong to him, because there is a suspicion that they are stolen" (*Mishneh Torah*, *Hilkhot Geneivah*, chap. 6, *halakhah* 9).

"It is forbidden to help the robber make changes in the article stolen so that he can then legally sell it. . . . One may not have any benefit from the robbery . . . so one may not ride on an animal that has been stolen" (*Mishneh Torah*, *Hilkhot Gezeilah*, chap. 5, *halakhah* 2).

The Codes all forbid nonpayment of taxes and evasion of customs duties levied by legitimate and accountable governments like those in most countries where Jews live today and classify such evasion as theft (*Mishneh Torah*, *Hilkhot Gezeilah VeAveidah*, chap. 5, *halakhot* 11–12). Buying goods on which taxes and customs were not paid seems to be forbidden according to the above *halakhot*.

"People who are known robbers [or thieves] or those whose wealth is regarded as having its source in theft . . . it is forbidden to have a benefit from them even for free . . . even to accept money for the charitable funds is forbidden. . ." (*Shulchan Arukh*, *HaRav Baal HaTanya*, *Hilkhot Gezeilah VeGeneivah*, sec. 12).

Postscript

"And I will draw close to you to judge [you] and I will be a swift witness against . . . the swearers to falsehood and against those that oppress the worker [through delay] of his wages, the widow, the orphan and pervert the rights of the stranger and [so] fear not Me" (Malachi 3:5).

9

חִלּוּל הַשֵּׁם

Chillul Hashem—By Desecrating God's Name

Any action that brings God's Name or His Chosen People, Israel, into disrepute is perhaps the most serious crime in Judaism. Economic misbehavior is one of the most common examples of this crime, spread by modern means of communication and the mass media to an extent unknown before in human history. Thus the desecratory effect of such immoral actions is multiplied. Jews involved in fraudulent bankruptcy, white collar crime, tax evasion, economic exploitation in whatever form, or Social Security fraud automatically contribute to defamation of His Holy Name, and the misdeed is made worse by the degree of Jewish identity, learning, or communal status of the culprits. Conversely when Jewish-owned corporations or individual businessmen conduct themselves scrupulously and in accordance with God's Law, they bring honor and sanctification both to the Jewish People and to He Who spoke and the world was.

"Neither shall you profane My Holy Name but I will be sanctified among the Children of Israel: I am the Lord Who makes you holy, Who brought you out of the land of Egypt to be your God" (Leviticus 22:32–33).

"The whole of Israel is commanded to sanctify His Name . . . and is warned against desecrating His Name even as it is written 'You shall not desecrate My Holy Name'" (*Mishneh Torah*, *Hilkhot Yesodei HaTorah*, chap. 5, *halakhah* 1).

"This is to be practiced in every place [in *Eretz Yisrael* and outside it] in every time by men and by women . . . and one who desecrates His Name transgresses heinously even as our Sages said [*Talmud Bavli*, *Yoma* 86a] 'There is nothing which cleanses this sin, neither repentance, nor Yom Kippur, nor affliction and suffering, but only death atones'" (*Sefer HaChinukh*, *mitzvah* 296).

"It is preferable that a [holy] letter should be erased from the Torah than that the Name of Heaven should be publicly profaned" (*Talmud Bavli*, *Yevamot* 79a).

"It is better to worship idolatry than to profane the Name of Heaven in public" (*Talmud Bavli*, *Sanhedrin* 107a).

"There is no credit for a person who profanes the Name, intentionally or unintentionally. What does it mean, there is no credit? Mar Zutra said: 'They do not act to him like a shopkeeper [who gives credit many times and then collects it all at once. In Heaven they do not act thus to those who profane the Name, but punishment is meted out immediately—Rashi]'" (*Talmud Bavli*, *Kiddushin* 40a).

"Moreover, even though there is no cure for this disease like there is for other sins, a person can find a cure if the Holy One, may He be exalted, helps him to sanctify His Torah in the eyes of people and to teach people the greatness of *Hashem* and the splendor of His Kingship" (*Rabbenu Yona*, *Shaarei Teshuvah*, *Shaar* 4:16).

"'All who hate Me love death' (Proverbs 8:36). Those who cause people to hate Me [through their unseemly actions] because they cause people to hate the Torah" (*Rabbenu Yona*, *Shaarei Teshuvah*, *Shaar* 3:113).

"The concept of desecrating God's Name . . . comes from the word *challal* (empty space), like emptying an area. So too here, it is as if the person who desecrates God's Name shows, God forbid, that the space that he stands in, is a country devoid of Him and that he does not worry about transgressing His commandments" (*Nefesh HaChaim*, *Shaar* 3, chap. 8).

"Everyone knows that this sin starts with something small and then rapidly expands . . . includes things that desecrate God and His commandments. . . . Who makes a false oath . . . also when people of stature and importance perform actions, [even those] that are not regarded as sins but through which the Torah and *mitzvot* [and thereby He Who commanded them and Israel to observe them] become cheapened in the eyes of others, this is called a desecration of His Name. It is obvious that the greater the stature of the perpetrator, the greater the sin: the higher the level in Torah, the more serious is his desecration" (Rabbenu Bachaya, *Kad HaKemech*, "*Chillul Hashem*").

What Is *Chillul Hashem*?

"Robbery from a non-Jew is more serious than robbery from a Jew because of the desecration of God's Name (*Tosefta*, *Bava Kamma* 10:15). The reason for this is that the latter case does not cause complaints [against Jews], nor does it give a bad name to the faith of Israel. But the one who steals from [or who exploits or wrongs in any way] a non-Jew causes complaints [against all Jews], gives a bad name to the faith of Israel and the Torah of Moses, and he thereby desecrates God's Name" (Rabbenu Bachaya, Commentary on the Torah, Leviticus 25:5).

"Abbaya says: 'As we learn in a *braita*—'And you shall love the Lord your God (Deuteronomy),' that the Name of Heaven should become beloved because of your actions [as when] a person learns *Chumash* and *Mishnah* and Talmud and he deals with people in gentleness . . . [*Rabbenu Channanell* substitutes 'And he deals with people in the marketplace in justice'] but someone who learns *Chumash* and *Mishnah* and Talmud but does not deal with people honestly in business and his relationships with people are not based on kindness [gentleness] then what will people say about him? Woe to so and so that he learned Torah! Woe to his father who taught him Torah! Woe to his rabbi who taught him Torah! . . . See how corrupted his actions are, see how ugly his ways are'!" (*Talmud Bavli*, *Yoma* 86a).

"Just as you have to act in good faith with Jews so too must you act in good faith with non-Jews. And if a non-Jew makes a mistake [in your favor and you do not put him right], be careful. He might find out afterward and then the Name of Heaven will be desecrated by your actions" (*Sefer Chasidim* 1080).

"This is particularly true of financial matters. It is imperative that in situations when there is even a one-in-a-thousand risk of desecrating God's Name, of theft, or evading even a tinge of a prohibition he should ascribe no value whatsoever to money. He should be strong and he should ignore the money [gold and silver] involved because it is better that he should die of hunger than be evil in the sight of God even for a moment. In our generation in particular, there is a need for the greatest care and caution . . . because the number of those who have rejected Judaism has grown and they are hungry for instances of Torah scholars and those who fear evil and meditate on His Name, erring . . ." (*Pele Yoetz*, *Chillul Hashem*).

"It is well known that much trouble has arisen in Jewish communities and settlements because of wicked people who engage in trade of counterfeit coins. As a result, instead of it being said, 'The remnant of Israel does no evil,' they [the gentiles] say, 'Where is the God of this nation [so demeaning Him]?' We have therefore agreed that from this day forth anyone found engaged in such activities shall be punished by Heaven; it shall be forbidden for any Jew to marry his daughter, or to give him lodging, or to call him to the Torah, or to allow him to fulfill any religious funding" (Synod of the Jews of German communities, Frankfurt, called by the rabbis of Germany, 1603).

"Anyone who borrows money or goods from gentiles with the intention of failing to pay for them shall also be ostracized, and no Jew shall buy any wares from him or do any business with him . . . so that the gentiles may know that our community is not guilty of such corrupt practices" (ibid.).

This necessity to protect the community against anti-Semitism and *chillul Hashem* whenever Jews were involved in financial scandals, deliberate or unintentional, led to an acceptance of such bans in all of the autonomous Jewish *kehillot*, which were, in fact, ministates. Because of the rabbinic partnership with the councils of such communities, the bans reflected halakhic rulings. The following is one of many bans related to bankruptcy.

"If a bankrupt debtor should offer to make a settlement for his debts with his creditors [bankruptcy], then a ban is to be published against him. For a whole year he is to be considered under the ban, unfit to bear testimony or to take an oath before the *bet din* . . . and shall not be called up to the Torah until he repays all his notes. The creditors may take away all the [festive] clothes he has made for his wife within the year in which he became bankrupt [halakhically they could take all his personal possessions, any jewels, and so on, except for his *tefillin*, a bed, food for thirty days, and so forth] . . . and shall lose the right of citizenship in the community. . . . When the ban is pronounced in the synagogue, the man's wife and children shall be present. . . . Whenever the leaders of any community will not carry out the ban they will have to pay a fine of 200 ducats [to the *Vaad Arba Aratzot*] which will not be refunded but used for *pidyon sh'vuyim*—redemption of captives . . . they will also be personally liable for the debts" (Council of the Four Lands—*Vaad Arba Aratzot*—Lublin, March 1624. This is basically an enactment of the *Shulchan Arukh, Choshen Mishpat*, sec. 97, subsec. 21 [see *Be'er HaGolah* for a halakhic sanction for these bans]).

What Is *Kiddush Hashem*?

"See how onerous is the sin of robbery, that two of the greatest of the Jews had to state clearly [that they had not abused their power and thereby caused a desecration of God in Whose Name they appeared]. . . . Moses said (Numbers 16:15), 'I did not take a single donkey in order to transport my belongings. I myself used my own donkey, harnessed it, and loaded my goods onto it even as it is written' (Exodus 4:18). And Moses took his wife and children. . . . Samuel too, after anointing Saul as king, challenged the people to claim whether he had ever 'taken anybody's ox or donkey, whether he had oppressed anybody, or taken a bribe from somebody to pervert justice'" (*Yalkut Shimoni*, Samuel 1:12).

"Shimon ben Shatach sent his disciples to buy a donkey from an idolater in Ashkelon. When they returned, they found a jewel in the halter bag of the donkey. They rejoiced, seeing this as an act of Divine Providence rewarding their teacher.

He, however, insisted that they return the jewel. When they did so, the idolater exclaimed, 'Blessed be the God of Shimon ben Shatach'" (*Talmud Yerushalmi*, *Bava Metziah*, chap. 4, *halakhah* 5).

"In all your ways you shall know Him" (Proverbs 3:6).

The Tribes of Israel were afraid to cross the Jordan into the Promised Land even though they were a pious generation. As long as they dwelled in the desert, ate manna from heaven, drank water from the miraculous well of Miriam, and were protected from the elements by the Clouds of Glory, they felt they were able to worship God and sanctify His Name. After crossing the Jordan, however, they would have to plow, sow, and reap. They would have to build houses and earn a livelihood through natural ways. Despite this, they still wanted to achieve holiness and sanctify His Name thereby. This type of sanctification they felt they were unable to achieve and therefore remained in the desert for forty years (*Shem MiShmuel Parshah Shlath*).

"And you shall love the Lord your God . . . with all your strength"—Rashi: "with all your possessions" (Deuteronomy 6:5).

It is written (Exodus 15:26), "If you will hearken to the voice of the Lord, your God, and do that which is honest [literally, "straight"] in His eyes, and carry out His commandments, and observe all His laws . . . that which is honest refers to buying and selling [actually, everything to do with money]. From this we learn that one whose commerce is in honesty and in faith, it is as though he observed the whole of the Torah" (*Mechilta*, *Shemot BeShalach*).

Adding to this the *Torah Temimah* writes, "This is because one is constantly faced with money temptations in commerce both regarding that which is between man and God and that which is between man and man. So if one is able to withstand them, he has great merit."

"Everyone whose commerce with others is in honesty and in faith, he expresses his faith in God Who is Truth" (*Ma'alot HaMidot*; *Emunah*).

"[So] the commerce of such a person becomes a crown to his head and the Name of Heaven is sanctified by him. . . . His work and his business are considered to be an act of charity [which similarly sanctifies God's Name in public], and it is as though he were busy with Torah and *mitzvot* as such commerce finds favor in God's eyes" (*Meam Lo'ez*, *Devarim*).

Postscript

"The Name of God which we bear is to be holy, the supreme Absolute in our midst. . . . Each time we refuse to devote so much as one impulse of our nature, one stimulus of our aspirations, one fiber of our being, one fragment of our possessions to the fulfillment of His Holy Will, we profane His Holy Name. We cause the Name . . . to become *challal*, a 'lifeless, powerless shell' . . . to the extent that others become aware of our sin against the Law of God, our invidious example becomes propaganda to demonstrate the impotence of the Name of God that rests upon us. By our sin we imply that one can call himself a Jew and be regarded as such, even if he abandons the obedience to God implicit in this Name as worth nothing compared to the first opportunity for sensual gratification, for personal pleasure or for material profit.

"Also, the more an individual stands out as an 'upholder of the Name of God' by virtue of his knowledge of the Word of God and his personal standing in the nation, the more imperative it is that he heed the command, 'Do not profane My Holy

Name.' In his case, even his slightest deviation, or semblance of deviation, from veracity and integrity, from morality and godly living, from the justice, goodness, and loving-kindness which the Law demands will become a gross act of *chillul Hashem*. . . . On the contrary, 'Let Me be sanctified in the midst of the sons of Israel.' God and His Holy Will are to be perceived and obeyed as the supreme, all-surpassing, all-commanding sanctum in every aspect of Jewish life, . . . our very lifeblood, all our urges and aspirations, the energies of our bodies, our nourishment, prosperity, and joy of living, upon the altar of God for the fulfillment of His Will" (S. R. Hirsch on Leviticus 22:32–33).

10

בְּיֵצֶר הָרָע

B'yetzer Hara—By the Ability to Do Evil

The *yetzer hara* ("evil inclination") for obtaining and retaining material wealth is probably one of the most powerful impulses people have. Still, money is not considered an evil in Judaism and like all the other evil inclinations can be used positively when controlled and educated by Torah and its *mitzvot*. Because of its very power, there are more commandments about achieving the education needed to "kosher" money (at least 120) than there are, for example, about kosher food.

"'Adam was cursed twofold when expelled from the Garden of Eden.' Sustenance [in Hebrew] is called *taraf*—insomuch as it has to be 'snatched' in the struggle with nature [however,] at the same time one has to struggle for existence against our fellowman—*lechem*, 'bread,' is the grammatical root of *milchamah*, 'war.' Did we not have to direct our minds so much to obtaining our daily bread, strife between man and man would not be so preeminent, and the idea of property would not weigh so heavily in the scales. . ." (S. R. Hirsch on Genesis 3:19).

The Talmud tells us regarding the sexual drive that "the more it has, the less it wants; the less it has, the more it wants" (*Talmud*

Bavli, Sukkah 42a). In regard to food, the less one has, the more one wants; the more one has, the less one wants. Money, however, is different to both of these. The less one has, the more one wants; the more one has, the more one wants. The rabbis told us, "A man has a hundred coins, yet wants two hundred" (*Midrash Rabbah*, *Kohelet* 1:34). "Nobody leaves this world with even half of his desires fulfilled" (*Talmud Bavli*).

"Alexander the Great once weighed a skull in the pans of a scale while in the other pan he placed gold, silver, and jewels. No matter how much was poured into the pan, the skull was heavier. Then, Alexander placed some dust in the eye sockets of the skull. Now finally [as in death] the scales rose and the money outweighed the skull" (*Talmud Bavli, Taanit*).

What drives this unlimited and seemingly unsatiated lust, which neither age nor illness nor plenty seems to weaken? The major factor seems to be the fear of uncertainty about having enough to protect us against the unknown future. If one would know what would happen to the markets, how long we would live, the status of our health, and what would happen to our children in the future, we would be free from the pressure to accumulate as much wealth as possible. While there is no objection to or evil in protecting ourselves through insurance, savings, and investment, as often as not the fear of uncertainty creates tremendous pressure to protect ourselves even in immoral and evil ways.

We constantly repeat the error of our fathers in the desert. When the manna came from Heaven, the Children of Israel were commanded to gather each day only what they needed—one *omer* for each person. Those who trusted in God did so, but those who had wants in addition to their needs or whose needs were unlimited gathered more. Nevertheless, at the end of the day, each had only what he really needed. More important, like all people, some of our fathers did not trust Moses or God; in case there might be no manna the next day, they illegally stole some extra. The punishment came swiftly. Our punishment is usually less obvious and more delayed but nevertheless ultimately comes: the extra turns wormy, inedible, and useless.

"The lesson that this whole procedure for gaining one's livelihood [for all generations] was: that which man hoards up [earns] against God's will in a miserly property-worshiping, God-denying spirit, God gives over to the worms and it becomes foul" (S. R. Hirsch on Exodus 17:11–21).

It is this which leads us to steal, to lie, to deny the right of others to a livelihood—to maximize profits and wealth. Concerning this we read 'One who pursues wealth is never satisfied' (*Kohelet* 5:9).

The attitude of the *halakhah* to the phenomenon of one-sided voiding of contracts is perhaps the clearest practical application of the lack of faith in God. "Rav Kahane received money for flax, and before delivery the price of the flax rose. He came to find out whether he could cancel the sale. . . . Rabbi Jochanan [whose opinion became law] ruled that this would be a lack of belief in God" (*Talmud Bavli*, *Bava Metziah* 49a).

The *Shulchan Arukh* rules accordingly "that one paid money [which in *halakhah* according to rabbinic decree does not constitute a sale of movable goods. This made the seller protect the goods until the buyer took possession] but did not take possession through a physical act. Even though legally there has not been a sale, whosoever wishes to change their mind, either buyer or seller, does an act which does not befit a Jew. He now becomes liable to a public curse in the form of *Mi Sheparah*. This is even if he only paid part of the price. One who sold goods verbally and agreed on the price, it is fitting that he fulfill his word. Even though he paid out no money or made no sign on the goods that they belonged to him, so that he does not deserve *Mi Sheparah,* still, whether buyer or seller retract, this is a lack of faith and the Sages disapproved" (*Choshen Mishpat*, sec. 4, subsec. 1 and 7).

This is the opinion of the Rambam as well. It is true that the Rama in his gloss, presenting the opinion of the Tur and Rosh, holds that in those cases where there has been a price change, voiding a verbal contract is not a lack of faith. However, still they hold that, as an act of righteousness, even here one should not renege.

"How is the *Mi Sheparah*—"He who demanded payment"—administered? The guilty party is cursed in the *bet din* saying, 'The Lord Who demanded payment from the generation of the Flood, from the people of the Tower of Babel, from the people of Sodom, and of the Egyptians who drowned in the Red Sea will surely punish one who does not keep his word'" (*Shulchan Arukh*, *Choshen Mishpat*, sec. 4, subsec. 4).

The Panim Meirot explains these references as examples of where God's punishment was publicized, since the whole world witnessed them. So too, those cases where human courts could not operate since no adjusted loss had occurred were publicly proclaimed in the assurance that they too would earn Divine punishment.

Faith as the Antidote for the Financial *Yetzer Hara*

The fear of uncertainty motivating so much business immorality and unethical behavior flows primarily from people's idea that their wealth is solely a function of their ability, luck, or hard work. The more they pursue wealth, the more the wealth increases; fear makes anything permissible. But although the world was created in such a fashion that our needs are fulfilled through nonmiraculous methods, it is an item of faith in Judaism that all wealth originates with God. There exists, therefore, a two-way relationship between human beings and the God who provides for them, a relationship that is materialistic and spiritual at the same time.

The snake was cursed in Genesis by having to eat of the dust of the earth. "What kind of punishment is this?" asked Menachem Mendel of Kotsk. "Dust is the most plentiful commodity in the world. Yes, but the Lord told the snake the whole world has a relationship to Me through My satisfaction of all their needs. You are accursed, take your livelihood, and get out of My sight."

Menachem Mendel's grandson, Shmuel of Sochochow, emphasized this lack of a relationship with the King of the Universe in our economic life. Although it was foretold that the sons of Abraham would be enslaved, no mention was made of where it would occur, so why was Egypt destined for our exile? "The whole world gets its rain, the source of existence, from Heaven. Men lift their eyes to Heaven, pray to God, and receive their bounty from His hand. In Egypt, however, all wealth comes from the Nile. There, men walk with their eyes on the ground, and there is no reciprocal relationship between the Divine and man. Israel had to serve in bondage in that place where no connection between Heaven and earth existed" (*Shem MiShmuel, Haggadah Shel Pesach*).

Just as self-made men cannot really be religious, all of us, when we forget the real source of our wealth, lack faith in Divine Providence. That faith is the major deterrent against our acts of fraud, theft, and oppression in all their variations. "[So] the first question a person is asked when he appears before the Heavenly Judge is 'Did you conduct your financial matters in faith, *be'emunah*?'" (*Talmud Bavli, Shabbat* 31a).

This is usually understood as relating to doing business in an honest and faithful manner. However, a more careful reading shows that what is involved is faith in God as the Provider of all needs, not only of mankind but also of all the creatures in the world. "All eyes turn to Thee and You give them their food in its season. He opens His hand and satisfies materially all living things completely" (Psalm 145:15–16). It is this faith knowing that He will provide, which enables us to face the uncertainty of the world in all spheres but especially in regard to monetary matters. Such knowledge is the real antidote for the fear that leads to crime, fraud, and oppression whereby people try to protect their wealth. Faith enables us to handle money, earning and spending morally and ethically, according to the Will of the Divine Provider. "And the righteous liveth by his faith" (Habakkuk 2:4).

"One whose commerce is *be'emunah* will not be tempted by the possibility of earning money through a falsehood. His faith will remind him of the Divine Provider's commands: 'Distance yourself from falsehood; you shall not defraud one another, and just weights and measures you shall have'" (*Kedushat Levi* 105).

"One who deals in faith [in both its meanings] cannot be sued to refund overcharging. This is when one says, 'I bought the goods for such a sum and this is my profit margin,' since he did not attempt to hide the price differential compared to the market price. At the same time he did not try to earn his money fraudulently, displaying faith that God would provide" (*Mishneh Torah*, *Hilkhot Mechirah*, chap. 13, *halakhah* 5).

"Rabbi Tanchum bar Abba proclaimed, 'A person of faith receives many blessings' (Proverbs 28). So one finds that those whose commerce is *be'emunah*, God brings blessings to the world through him [God promised Abraham that he would be a blessing for the world (Genesis 22:18)]. However, those who cannot be trusted and those of little faith who strive to become wealthy will not be cleansed" (*Shemot Rabbah* 51a).

Educating the *Yetzer Hara*

The *yetzer hara* is often translated as "evil impulse," which would make it akin to original sin or to a power that people's free will cannot control or alter. In the light of Judaism's insistence that the *yetzer hara* can indeed be educated and made holy, it would seem better to regard it as the ability or desire to do evil. Since the *yetzer hara* for money is so powerful, our Sages saw in it not only a spiritual challenge but also an opportunity of the first magnitude for achieving holiness. "He who wishes to achieve the level of righteousness, let him conduct himself according to all the monetary laws [of Judaism]" (*Talmud Bavli*, *Bava Kamma* 30a). Furthermore, these laws of commerce, finance, and industry usually called *nezikin* (literally, "damages") the Sages called by an alternative name—the Book of Redemption (*Talmud Bavli*, *Shabbat* 31a). The human being can achieve salvation through observing these monetary laws.

"When one is busy with his profession, [work or business] he should not think he is free of Torah and permitted everything. For this the Psalmist says, 'My friend is faith' (Psalm 37:3), that is, you should be strong and make sure that all your acts are done *be'emunah* [in honesty]. . . . Join yourself to faith and you will find that the honesty attaches itself to you, since it includes all of the 613 *mitzvot*" (Ramban, *Emunah VeHaBitachon*, chap. 1).

Thus the study of the divinely revealed Torah in all its ramifications is the prerequisite of sanctifying and educating the *yetzer hara* for money. "It is commendable for Torah study to be combined with *derekh eretz* [here understood to refer to earning a livelihood] since joint achievement discourages sin"

(*Avot*, chap. 2, *mishnah* 2). The achievement of a livelihood diminishes fraud and crime while the Torah knowledge provides the blueprint of sanctity and righteousness in material things.

"Every man in Israel is obligated to study Torah, irrespective of whether he is rich or poor, ill or in good bodily health, young or old . . . he is obligated to devote time in the day and in the night . . . those who cannot learn [an intellectual shortcoming] and those who are preoccupied with earning a living should assist others to learn" (*Shulchan Arukh*, *Yoreh De'ah*, sec. 246, subsec. 1).

Yosef Karo's exemptions hardly apply to the vast majority of businesspeople today, who possess intellectual ability. The preoccupation with a livelihood in our modern age of prosperity, one unprecedented in human history, is a drive that is self-induced and therefore controllable.

This obligation to a lifelong study of God's Word reduces the time available for business and thereby the want for an ever-rising standard of living, with the immoral pressures this brings. At the same time, the knowledge of permitted and forbidden actions, together with the demands of justice and mercy, creates an ideological framework for an ethical and moral economy.

"Rebbe [Rabbi Yehuda HaNasi, redactor of the *Mishnah*] said, 'What is the perfect path one should follow? . . . There are those who say he should grasp excessive faith [Rashi: He should conduct his business with people in faith and not defraud them] as it is written: The Lord's eyes are upon the faithful of the earth, to dwell in His presence'" (*Talmud Bavli*, *Tamid* 28a).

"What should a person do in order to become wealthy? [Rabbi Yehoshua ben Chananyah said to the people of Alexandria] 'He should earn his livelihood faithfully.' They questioned this, saying that many had tried this but had failed. He replied 'One should pray for mercy from He Who is the source of wealth.' What is the meaning [of earning a livelihood honestly if everything is dependent on the mercy of Heaven]? To teach us that we require both of them" (*Talmud Bavli*, *Niddah* 70b).

This requirement is clearly spelled out in the laws pertaining to our daily behavior, as they appear in all the Codes. After some 145 sections relating to rising up in the morning, washing one's hands, *tallit*, *tefillin*, and the order of the morning prayers, the laws include a section on business conduct in general, over and above the codex contained in *Choshen Mishpat*. After preparing the body and the mind through spiritual meditation and preparation comes the application. So, "After this [morning prayer] one should go to one's daily business, make that a restricted priority, and study of Torah a major one [limiting his activity and thus the race for an ever-spiraling standard of living]. All his actions should be in honesty and good faith" (*Shulchan Arukh*, *Orach Chaim*, sec. 146).

Postscript

The Lord promised Abraham that when his children left their exile [Egypt] they would go out with the wealth of their country. This could not have meant much to Abraham who refused to take even a shoelace from the King of Sodom, whom he had rescued from captivity. Later the Lord told Moses that after they left Egypt they would worship Him at Sinai and receive the Torah. This was the real promise to Abraham. The Children of Israel would receive great wealth, but also God's Torah to teach them how to use it honestly, righteously, and clean of any evil. So the *yetzer hara* would be sanctified.

11

בְּיוֹדְעִים וּבְלֹא יוֹדְעִים

B'yodim U'v'lo Yodim—Wittingly and Unwittingly

People do not deliberately and consciously set out to rob, defraud, or damage their fellowman. Rather they tend to rationalize deceitful behavior, making witting acts into seemingly unwitting ones. Further, the ethical climate surrounding us, which accepts the prevailing lax moral standards, the development of gray areas in morality, and the socially pervasive pressure for an ever-higher standard of living all help to blur the distinction between permitted and forbidden actions. Man created in the image of God possesses free will and therefore is always responsible for his actions.

"If a person who sins and does any of those things which God forbade, but he is not certain [either that it is forbidden or that he actually did it], yet he is guilty and has to bear his iniquity. Rabbi Akiva reading this verse [in Leviticus 5:17] would burst into tears saying, 'If one who intended to eat fat [which is permitted] but ate forbidden fat [*chalev*] is regarded as guilty by the Torah, how much more so would one be who deliberately ate forbidden fat'" (*Talmud Bavli, Kiddushin* 81b).

"A human being is always liable [to pay full compensation for damage done] irrespective of whether it is caused deliberately or inadvertently and irrespective of whether it is caused while he is asleep or while he is awake" (*Mishnah Bava Kamma*, chap. 2, *mishnah* 6).

Evading responsibility for one's actions is the beginning of unethical behavior in business. Acquiescence in widespread practices, thievery from one's employer or from government agencies and insurance companies, and negligence either in one's job or agency or regarding the environment are the natural consequence of *Yodim velo yodim*.

The Corporate Veil

The corporation emerged as a means of limiting shareholders' liability to their equity in the company and as a way of protecting private assets from being seized by creditors. Today, however, treating the corporation as a separate entity divorced from the personality of the shareholders has created a veil between the moral behavior of the corporation and the ethical demands placed on the shareholders. It is difficult to assess the ethical preferences of shareholders in large corporations and so the directors feel that their obligation is only to earn the highest profit relative to considerations of risk and capital growth. In privately held corporations the corporate veil permits actions against other shareholders and customers and misdeeds like tax evasion, which often differ radically from the morality considered appropriate for the officers as individuals. The veil enables all concerned, shareholders and executive officers, to pollute the environment, evade safety regulations, and defraud without feeling that they have compromised their personal morality. Employees too think that stealing from a corporation by using its equipment for personal needs, by not performing their jobs properly, or by using for private gain information learned in the course of their work are acceptable acts; insider trading, for example, often results from using of such information, as does speculation on their own account by traders or agents.

Although halakhically there seems to be no difficulty with the limited-liability nature of the corporation (*Mishneh Halakhot*, vol. 6, sec. 277), Judaism permits no corporate veil for evading the moral responsibilities flowing from ownership of wealth. Corporations with a majority of Jewish shareholders are required to sell their *chometz* before Pesach and may not operate on *Shabbat* (*Elef LeShlomo*, sec. 238; *Minchat Yitzchak*, pt. 3, sec. 1, pt. 4, secs. 17–18; *Iggrot Moshe, Orach Chaim*, pt. 1, sec. 52, subsec. 3). Corporate officers, shareholders, and employees, therefore, would seem to be obliged to follow the *halakhot* regarding business as well as the *lifnim mishurat hadin*—beyond the requirements of the law—that pertain to the individual.

Socially Acceptable Immorality

As often as not, employees' use of company stationery or telephones for private purposes is considered permissible both because the monetary amounts are usually small and because in many societies such practices are commonly not perceived to be immoral. The same reasoning of social acceptability often permits us to make false claims for insurance, Social Security, and other funds, even though the sums involved are much larger.

"It is forbidden according to the Torah to steal anything [*kol shehu,* just as leavened bread (*chometz*) is forbidden on Pesach in even the smallest amount]. This is forbidden even in jest, even with the intention of later returning the stolen goods [usually the avowed intention of embezzlers]. It is even forbidden when the purpose is only to annoy the owner. Everything is forbidden so that theft should not become habitual [through repetitive acts not perceived as theft]" (*Shulchan Arukh, Choshen Mishpat*, sec. 348, subsec. 1).

"Anything which is taken without the permission of the owner is theft" (*Mishneh Torah*, *Hilkhot Geneivah VeAveidah*, chap. 1, *halakhah* 3).

Commenting on the *Mishnah* in *Avot* (chap. 5, *mishnah* 18), where "Ben Teimah says . . . as powerful as a lion to do the will of your Father in Heaven, many Sages have pointed out that although modesty and forebearing are the signs of the Jew, there are times when one requires to be strong and outspoken against evil." Furthermore, "A person should always know that all his actions are evident before the Great King, even those conducted in private and in secrecy. . . . He should remember that He whose glory fills the whole world stands above him and sees all his deeds. Then the person will immediately be filled with fear, humble himself before God [and refrain from doing anything that God forbade], and ashamed before Him [whenever he does something evil] (*Guide to the Perplexed*, pt. 3, chap. 22). So one should never have fear or be ashamed before those people who mock at the service of God" (Rama, *Orach Chaim*, sec. 1, subsec. 1).

"In our time for our many sins, the number of voices providing justification for actually taking from one's fellows have expanded and therefore breaches [in the form of theft] even without any attempt at justification have multiplied. This is particularly true of the illegal use of [Social Security and other] benefits whether in regard to grants, loans, and services. People are especially prone to provide justification for unethical acts against organizations and corporations, for example, health insurance funds and insurance firms. This in addition to the theft involved also requires false declarations [which transgress 'You shall separate yourself from falsehood']. It is also true that if a person has a right to receive goods or services free of charge or at a discount [frequent flyer credits, food stamps or mortgages, and credit available only to special groups of people, which actually constitutes subsidized credit] and uses that privilege for things that he is not meant to or for other people, that constitutes theft" (*Pitchei Choshen*).

"One should not ask anyone for a present because they may acquiesce out of embarrassment [or out of fear in the case of employees or small suppliers] and then it will be theft. It is even forbidden to borrow one's friend's book to learn Torah from without his permission [seemingly harmless and for a good cause]; a person intends to do a *mitzvah* [just like those who see their charitable donations as an alibi for their stealing] and ends up doing a sin. The same is even truer with someone who does not want to give the object; to take from him is outright theft" (*Pele Yoetz* 300, *Shoel Shelo Mida'at*).

"The principle is: every sin which is more prevalent and is more easily perpetrated involves greater punishment. [So too when the party involved is a famous person, wealthy, or a scholar, the punishment is greater.] For example, when one steals a sheep, he pays a fine equal to the theft whereas others, for example a robber or one who denies a debt or, receiving trust money, only gives back the object stolen [and under certain circumstances a 20 percent fine]. This is because the sheep graze in the fields and it is difficult to guard over them, while cattle do not ever graze in groups; in both cases theft is relatively easy. Robbery, however, is rarer and more difficult, so the guilty person is not liable to pay double the value of the goods" (*Moreh Nevuchim*, pt. 3, chap. 41).

This would seem to indicate a rising scale of punishment depending on the position of a person in the corporate hierarchy that enables him to steal, defraud, or oppress. More easily supervised, lower echelons would find such acts more difficult and therefore should be leniently treated. The same scale applies to professionals whose knowledge of the law, of quality control, or of financial markets makes it easier to defraud those they are advising or those to whom they are selling.

All too often we witness people doing immoral acts in the name of a socially just, meritorious cause. Animal rights activitists who destroy other people's property or their livelihoods, pro-life supporters who commit arson or mayhem and kill pro-abortionists, academics who falsify research results, or software experts who disguise bugs in their programs in order to obtain funds for research projects are only some examples of people operating according to the maxim "The end justifies the means." So too, lay leaders of charitable or educational institutions, faced with budgetary shortfalls, are often tempted to falsify the numbers of students or patients in order to obtain government funding, while the advertised suffering of those in their care is not always accurately or truthfully described.

From a responsum of Rabbi Moshe Feinstein in our generation, it is clearly not permissible to take government money illegally or fraudulently, irrespective of the sanctity or importance of the purpose for which it is to be used. Furthermore, the rabbi sees these actions as being theft, *geneivat daat,* and active lying while creating a *chillul Hashem*, desecrating God's Name, as well as being an insult to Torah and its students. He concludes, "There is no *heter* for it" (*Iggrot Moshe*, *Choshen Mishpat*, pt. 2, sec. 29).

The excerpt from the *Shulchan Arukh* quoted previously, forbidding theft in all its forms, includes such misguided unethical behavior: "Even to become obligated to pay the four- and fivefold fines mandatory for one who stole a sheep or an ox and slaughtered them." "The motive for such a theft is to please the owner when one knows that he will refuse to take a gift" (Rashi, *Bava Metziah* 41b).

Negligence and Carelessness

When one is not careful to prevent one's property doing damage to another person's health or property, one is committing a sin, *belo yodin*, unintentionally yet a sin for which compensation must be paid. Furthermore, the offender is halakhically obligated to actively remove articles or objects that can cause harm to others even if they lie on public property. In this respect, it must be remembered that the classic categories of damages like the goring ox or the pit in a public thoroughfare are easily translated into their modern versions. For example, the immovable pit that causes a person to collide with it is similar to a vehicle parked at night without lights or an automobile double-parked where it should not be. Industrial pollution, noisy factories, smell, and toxic waste, which are forbidden by *halakhah,* are applicable today in business as they were in the following sources. Over and above monetary compensation, we are enjoined to prevent such damage, even if we later agree to pay the compensation.

"The question concerns a *Cohen* who caused a fatal accident while driving his car. Is he still permitted after this to participate in the customary *birkat Cohanim* [the priestly blessings recited in the Land of Israel every day, but in the diaspora only on festivals]? The *Cohen* in our case may not recite the blessing since his driving caused a loss of life. Either he drove at excess speed, did not obey the traffic signal, or disobeyed some traffic regulations. His negligence became thereby a deliberate fatal action. An accuser [a murderer] cannot become an advocate [the priest asking for a blessing of peace]. In the case of the motor car, its high speed is liable to cause even greater damage [than the horse in the responsa of the Rosh, sec. 101, subsec. 5, on which this modern responsa is based], and his ability to stop suddenly is even less. The motor car is a major vehicle of potential damage. One who does not drive carefully is considered reckless. [The Rosh calls him a criminal who causes damage with his body, the horse being considered part of him] and like one who kills with his own hands" (*HaRav Ovadiah Yoseph*, *Yechaveh Daat*, pt. 5, sec. 6).

"One who performs . . . work which causes dust, smog, and similar [pollutants] is obligated to distance [his plant] . . . [even if the damage is not the direct result of the technological process], he is still obligated to distance [his plant from the city] in order to prevent [the pollution] from causing damage" (*Shulchan Arukh*, *Choshen Mishpat*, sec. 155, subsec. 34).

Usually a person can acquire a legal right—*chazakah*—if neighbors or an owner of a certain property do not protest actions like trespass or an economic undertaking. However, "There is no *chazakah* for four types of damage [so that even if those suffering did not complain for a long period and even if they actually agreed previously, the perpetrator can be forced to relocate]: smoke pollution, smell of sewage, dust, and the tremors caused by the pounding of machinery on the ground. . . . So too the damage caused to one's privacy does not have a *chazakah*. . . . This is because a person is unable to suffer these environmental damages and he always has a status that he does not waive his rights against them [One can also claim that 'At first I thought I could live with them but now I find I cannot']" (*Mishneh Torah*, *Hilkhot Shecheinim*, chap. 11, *halakhah* 4, and *Shulchan Arukh*, *Choshen Mishpat*, sec. 155, subsec. 41–43).

The rabbis included in this ruling one who, after opening a business in his house, causes the neighbors to object that the noise of customers coming and going keeps them awake.

"It is a positive *mitzvah* to erect a fence on the roof of one's house (Deuteronomy 22:8). One who does not do so desecrates a positive commandment and transgresses a negative one, as it is written, 'You shall not put blood in your house.' This applies to everything which is a potential source of danger to life. So if one has a well or pit in his courtyard, irrespective of whether it has water in it or not, they have to erect a fence around it or cover it adequately. . . . So too we are obligated to remove any obstacle which can cause fatal damage" (*Mishneh Torah*, *Hilkhot Roze'ach uShmirat HaNefesh*, chap. 11, *halakhot* 1–4).

"It is forbidden to cause damage to the [person or] property of another. [The *Shulchan Arukh*] commences with classifying damage as a forbidden act and only then goes on to rule that compensation is necessary. This is to teach us that even when the one causing the damage is prepared to pay compensation [as in the case where the cost of relocating a polluting plant or business or installing pollution preventive measures is greater than the cost of compensation], it is still forbidden. The same principle also applies to all the cases of theft and fraud" (*Meirat Einayim*, *Choshen Mishpat*, sec. 378, subsec. 1).

Just how seriously *halakhah* regards the guilt of performing actions that might be regarded as accidental may be seen from the following responsa, *teshuvah*, of Rabbi Akivah Eiger. The case concerned a person who had forced a laden cart to speed at night; as a result his son and an attendant were killed while sleeping on the loaded cart. It is particularly pertinent to modern industrial accidents that lead to a loss of life.

The man was a major cause [of what occurred] . . . what he did was [actually] close to *p'shiah*, intentional: he ran the horses loaded up at night. . . . The start of his repentance has to be that since his son and the attendant were killed and will not have any offspring, he must raise up children in their place. For his own son he has to calculate what he would have spent on the wedding [clothes and dowry included], and that sum must be put into a perpetual [trust] fund. The income must be used to support and educate a poor student until the age of 15 . . . and at that point he must do the same for another student. And he must call these students by the name of his son. . . . For the young attendant [presumably an employee] he must accept upon himself the obligation to pay every year for the education of poor children. In the first year he must also pay for ten poor teachers who will teach a class every day for the soul of those who were killed and will say the text of the prayers and *Kaddish deRabbanan*. He must also designate some of the profits [of the trust fund] to pay for people to learn *mishnayot* and to pray for the dead on the anniversary of their deaths. On that day he must send a *minyan* to their graves to plead with the dead to forgive him.

For three years he should fast every Monday and Thursday, the day before every *Rosh Chodesh*, "new moon." . . . He may replace the fast when traveling with a gift of money to the poor, three times eighteen [*chai*]. He may not go to a wedding banquet all his life [excepting his own children or if he is a best man]. Every night he should confess with a broken heart. . . and should beg for forgiveness from Hashem. . . . (*Teshuvot Rabbi Akiva Eiger*, no. 3)

Postscript

"Reflect upon three things and you will not come to commit a transgression. Know what is above you—a seeing eye, a hearing ear and all your deeds written [in His] Book" (*Mishnah Avot*, chap. 2, *mishnah* 1).

12

בְּכַפַּת שֹׁחַד

B'khapat Shochad—By Bribery

The primary form of bribery is influencing the judicial system, which distorts a process that Judaism views as one of the Divine attributes. In the marketplace, however, other forms of bribery create the same distortion by moving wealth from one person or group to another, contrary to Torah justice. In the modern state, the government is usually the major consumer, and its officials possess semijudicial powers in awarding contracts or evaluating tenders. Licenses, fines, and levies assessed or monitored by local or central government officials also are open to bribery. Such bribery demoralizes not only the recipient but also the giver; it is not the mouse that steals but the hole!

"And no bribery shall you take, for bribery blindeth those that see clearly and makes the words of just men flexible" (Exodus 23:9).

"You shall not distort judgment, neither shall you recognize faces [respect persons either powerful or weak] and shall take no bribes, for bribery blinds the eyes of wise men and makes the decisions of the righteous waver" (Deuteronomy 16:19).

"Cursed be he that takes bribes to slay a person of innocent blood. And all the people shall say 'amen'" (Deuteronomy 27:25).

The Judiciary

"It is a positive biblical [as distinct from rabbinical] *mitzvah* to appoint judges and executive officers [to implement the judicial decisions]" (*Mishneh Torah, Hilkhot Sanhedrin*, chap. 1, *halakhah* 1).

"Six commandments were given to Adam. . . . And laws [to appoint judges to implement the other *mitzvot* obligatory on Noachides. Nachmanides includes in this *mitzvah* also all the monetary obligations applicable to Jews (Genesis 34:13)]" (*Mishneh Torah, Hilkhot Melakhim*, chap. 9, *halakhah* 1).

The establishment of an equitable and just legal system is thus a religious requirement for both Jews and non-Jews. Such a requirement seems to be simply an essential arrangement for a viable human society, but close examination shows that it is really an application of *Imitatio Dei*, the striving in Judaism for human beings to emulate their Creator, Who is the King of Justice. This striving requires a legal system devised on principles beyond human conception and flowing from a divine revelation at Sinai. "Justice, justice, shall you pursue in order that you may live and inherit the land that the Lord your God gives to you" (Deuteronomy 16:20).

"The divine social laws are to be distinguished both from the Noachide laws and from those [developed from human intelligence] of other nations, in two significant ways. In the first instance they introduce concepts unknown and unknowable in human legislation [which makes the Torah social laws far more moral and far more extensive]. Secondly, these laws are subject to divine supervision, reward and punishment. . . . Human legislation has as its purpose only the consensus aimed at regulating the affairs of the state and society, thus reflecting only the egoistical desires of that society. [Divine law, however, provides normative and unchanging moral standards aimed at sanctifying human socio-political systems.]" (Abarbanel on the Torah, *Shemot* 21:1).

The concept of the absolute equity and justice of a divinely revealed law, among other things, lies behind the insistence of all the Codes that Jews refrain from recourse to non-Jewish courts or even Jewish ones that do not rule according to that law. Such recourse, in addition to desecrating the Name, may lead to a transfer of wealth in contradiction to *halakhah* , which in effect is an act of theft.

"It is forbidden [for Jewish parties to a case] to appear before a non-Jewish court or to be judged according to their laws. This applies even where non-Jewish courts decide according to *halakhah* and even if all the parties agree. Anyone who does any of these is called evil, and it is as though they cursed and blasphemed against the Torah of Moshe. If, however, the non-Jews insist [and refuse to allow the Jews autonomous courts, which many communities maintained for centuries] or if the other party is violent [and refuses to obey the rabbinic court] so that it is impossible to save the injured party's money from him through the imposition of Jewish law, he must first be summoned to the rabbinic court, and if he refuses [to come or to obey the judgment] then the courts will give permission to save his property through recourse to the regular court system" (*Shulchan Arukh, Choshen Mishpat*, sec. 26, subsec. 1–2).

Until the end of the eighteenth century in Western Europe and even later in Eastern Europe and the Middle East, Jewish recourse to autonomous courts administering halakhic justice was a norm. This independent judiciary existed even though communities lacked any police or physical force to administer their rulings. There was and is, however, a powerful social pressure that gives the *batei din* the "teeth" without which the whole system could easily become a travesty of justice. This pressure may be instituted even in the modern open societies in which we live.

"And these are the acts for which a person, male and female, is to be excommunicated and set aside . . . one who insults the agent of the court . . . one who refuses to appear before the *bet din* . . . one who refuses to accept the ruling of the rabbinic court. . . ." (*Mishneh Torah, Hilkhot Talmud Torah*, chap. 6, *halakhah* 14).

"One who is excommunicated is forbidden to cut his hair or wash his clothes [marks of mourning]; he may not be counted as a quorum for grace after meals, nor as part of a *minyan*. . . . If he dies during the period of excommunication, no eulogy is recited over him nor does anyone accompany his coffin to the grave . . . no one may hire him nor may he hire anybody . . . neither shall anybody trade with him or do any business with him except that which is essential to keep him alive" (*Mishneh Torah*, *Hilkhot Talmud Torah*, chap. 7, *halakhot* 4–5).

Even though there has long been no use of the *herem* in its strict legal sense, many similar strictures have been used over the centuries. Rabbinic courts and communities have the moral power to act against those who refuse to appear before the courts or to accept their decisions. The judicial decisions have included removal from communal office or honors such as being called to the reading of the Law, nonparticipation of the community in family celebrations of that person, and communal refusal to eat of his food. Such social pressure is usually more effective, in all societies, Jewish and otherwise, than prison sentences or fines not supported by public opinion.

Bribery

"The judge must be extremely careful not to take bribes even to justify the innocent. If he did so, he has to return the bribe if the giver demands it [he has to return it even if it is not claimed in order to be clear before Heaven (*Arukh HaShulchan*)]; . . . and the giver of the bribe transgresses the negative commandment of *lifnei iver*—a stumbling block in the path of the blind. Not only is monetary bribery forbidden but even verbal forms [such as flattery], and the judge is even enjoined from borrowing anything [from the litigant]" (*Shulchan Arukh, Choshen Mishpat*, sec. 9, subsec. 9).

"The above language of the *Shulchan Arukh*—very, very careful—*me'od me'od*, is also used by the Tur, and I wrote in my commentary there, that this is because of power of human coveting and the strong attraction for other people's money. This repetitive language is used by the Tur regarding the law of interest and regarding medicine. The latter since one must be exceedingly careful in matters affecting life and death. [*Me'od me'od*] is also used regarding sexual immorality" (*Meirat Einayim, Choshen Mishpat*, sec. 9, subsec. 9).

"The Hebrew word *shochad* is related to *shochet* [to slaughter] and *shicheit* [to destroy]. From this we get the basic idea of its meaning 'to bring about the destruction of the spiritual and moral force of somebody.'. . . Bribery blinds the sight of one who otherwise sees clearly . . . it does not [make the judge] so much crooked [but rather] faltering or unstable . . . not as clear and firm and decisive as he should be in giving expression to what is right" (S. R. Hirsch on Exodus 23:8).

Bribery may take many nonfinancial forms that equally distort justice and are as forbidden as monetary bribes. "You shall do no wrong in judgment. Grant no consideration to the poor [literally, 'to one in reduced circumstances'], neither show honor [in judgment] to the great; according to what is just, you shall judge your neighbor" (Leviticus 19:15).

"The first injunction is to the community not to misuse the position which the institution of the law courts gives it over individuals, by force or caprice. [There can be] misuse of the framing of these laws or even only vexatious dragging out which is the wrong in judgment [referred to in the Torah]" (S. R. Hirsch on Leviticus 19:15). This passage describes the *naval berishut ha'Torah*, an evil person exploiting the legal rulings. The prophet Amos (2:6) rallied against those who sell the poor for a pair of shoes. Rashi comments that the rich *na'alu* [the same Hebrew root as "shoe," but meaning "to lock in"] bought up all the fields around the poor person and then forced him to sell his field to them. Such an act is legal, but nevertheless a perversion of justice.

Our Sages saw the sin of the people of Sodom as being the legalization of evil and immoral acts. Acting on the legal principle that one is liable only if one steals a *shaveh prutah*, something of value, they perverted justice. Each man, woman, and child took one bean from a storekeeper's inventory until nothing was left. Nobody could be legally prosecuted, yet all were guilty of theft. When modern corporations hide behind a maze of straw companies or daughter corporations, they often do the same. For example, a drug developed by a daughter corporation may cause damage far in excess of the equity of that corporation. Claims for compensation from the injured parties may be severely limited, and at the same time the equity of the parent corporation may be legally shielded from any claims to supplement the compensation. This act may be legal, yet it is very similar to the acts of Sodom.

A similar distortion of justice happens when judges are able to be bribed by increases in their staff of clerks and secretaries or even by using their power to complicate the judicial process. "Every judge that enhances his office so that he may increase the wages [or the number] of his officials [who call the litigants to court] or his clerks is considered as one who lusts after bribes, and this is what the sons of Samuel did even as it is written 'they lusted after wealth and took bribes'" (1 Samuel 8:3) (*Mishneh Torah, Shoftim*, chap. 23, *halakhah* 3).

Rabbi Avraham of Sochochow, the *Avnei Nezer*, was once offered a bribe. He called his sons into the room and laid the money out on the table. "Why," remarked one of them, "they look like all the other coins." "That's the problem," said Rabbi Avraham. "It is because bribe money looks like any other money that it is easy to succumb to taking it." The same chasidic master once excused himself from sitting as a judge in a particular case. He explained that one of the litigants, a widow, came to see him and then burst into tears. "There is no greater bribery than the tears of a widow."

Beyond the Judiciary

"And not only a judge is forbidden to take bribes [and the giver forbidden to give them, a stumbling block in the path of the blind] but also all the officials and all those engaged in communal affairs. Even though their decisions are not specifically divine Torah, Torah laws, still they are not allowed to distort their decisions on a basis of favoritism or personal bias. They are definitely not allowed to take bribes" (*Arukh HaShulchan, Choshen Mishpat*, sec. 9, subsec. 1).

"Referring a matter of tenant–landlord relationship to a municipal inspector in New York is tantamount to recourse to a non-Jewish court since he fulfills a judicial role [This would make a bribe to the same inspector tantamount to bribing a judge]" (*Mishneh Halakhot*, vol. 4, sec. 113).

"We do not allow the king or the high priest to be included in the court that decides on declaring a leap year [the addition of the month of *Adar* II in order to equalize the lunar and solar calendars, seven times in a nineteen-year cycle]. The king is not allowed to participate because of his army. [The inclusion of an additional month meant extra costs for his treasury in order to pay salaries and supply his army. Since this was against his economic interest, his inclusion in the court would lead to a distortion of its rulings.] The high priest was not included because [of the problem] of the cold. [Here too a personal benefit was involved. On the Day of Atonement, all his work in the Temple was done barefoot and involved a number of ritual immersions. So he had a personal interest that it should be as warm as possible. Adding another month to the calendar meant Yom Kippur was a month closer to the Jerusalem winter]" (*Talmud Bavli, Sanhedrin* 18b).

This susceptibility to bribery of those in power was clearly understood by our Sages as may be seen from this talmudic discussion. "Regarding the sons of Eli the High Priest we are told, 'They lay with the women that assembled at the door of the Tabernacle' (1 Samuel 2:22). . . . Knowing that the share of the priests from the doves brought by the women as sin offerings were meager, the sons of Eli delayed them. They hoped that during this period, people would bring oxen and fattened calves from which their share would be more substantial. In this act of greed, they prevented the women from returning to their husbands, tantamount to adultery" (*Talmud Bavli, Yoma* 9a).

So, too, the Sages saw the accusation of the Bible referred to by Maimonides in the preceding section, that the sons of Samuel took bribes as being far more subtle than mere gross immorality. The accusation is thus far more pertinent to our own sophisticated economy. In most Western societies, people in positions of authority in local government, regulatory authorities, central government, and large corporations shy away from taking outright bribery, both because of the legal consequences and because society frowns upon blatant criminality. Subtle forms of influence, however, are extremely common, such as awarding contracts for public works in exchange for political contributions or gifts to family members, employment for officials after they leave public service, and favors gained from lobbyists. "The sons of Samuel, in their lust for money, forced the traders to do business on their behalf, they took by force [halakhic robbery] more than their share of the tithes [tax money?] or forced people to give them their tithes and priestly gifts rather than allowing them to choose freely [to whom they wished to give them as dictated by *halakhah*]" (*Talmud Bavli, Shabbat* 56a).

Whether bribing authorities is considered halakhic bribery or an indirect form of theft, it is still immoral. Such payments assure unfair advantage and cause financial damage to competitors or to the taxpaying citizen. The modern marketplace, because of the international and national scope of business, together with the extensive direct and indirect intervention of all levels of government in all aspects of commerce and finance, is riddled with opportunities and temptations for bribery. These easily transform marginal theft and robbery into corruption, which by becoming pervasive and common, is difficult to avoid. Paying an officer to avoid a fine for a traffic violation, buying information from stockbrokers or lawyers about impending mergers or changes in corporate earnings, and bribing government officials or elected politicians to obtain contracts or changes in zoning laws are only some examples of the grease that all too often oils the machinery of business. Western Europe and Japan have recently been rocked by scandals involving senior political figures taking illegal contributions from industrialists and financial factors in exchange for economic favors. The former Soviet Union and most socialist countries evolved systems of bribery to avoid the straitjacket of their planned economies. Such systems parallel the kickbacks, illegal commissions, and political lobbying of their counterparts in the free market economies. For good reason the United States adopted a foreign corrupt practices act that makes it illegal for corporations to pay any form of bribe even in those countries where it is normal business practice to do so.

All these immoral practices are meant to achieve the same effect as the judicial bribe. They are meant to blind the eyes of the wise, appointed or hired to monitor economic decisions, and to make the wisdom of the righteous, elected or appointed to protect society's or business's economic welfare, waver in the direction of the giver.

It is not the mouse that steals but the hole.

Postscript

"Love truth and justice and cleave to them, for in them lies your success. You will then be like one who builds on a strong rock. Despise falsehood and injustice and do not covet their savory delicacies, for you will then be like one who builds or plasters with saliva. A life of truth and justice should be more acceptable even if it appears to be less profitable than one of falsehood and wickedness. Buy the truth and sell it not" (Proverbs 23:23) (*The Last Will and Testament of Moses Maimonides*).

13

בְּכַחַשׁ וּבְכָזָב

B'KHACHASH U'V'KHAZAV—BY DENIAL AND BY FALSEHOOD

A major form of business immorality is the denial of contracts, verbal or written, or of obligations about prices, quality, and dates of performance. Falsehood is the common characteristic of deceptive advertising, exploiting another's ignorance or naïveté, and providing substandard work or services.

"If a person sins and behaves unfaithfully against God in that he denies to his neighbor a deposit which was made with him or a loan or something that he has robbed or something that he obtained by oppression or failed to return, something which was lost and denies it and swears falsely regarding anything that a person does, sinning thereby" (Leviticus 5:21–22).

"Any dishonesty in affairs between man and man is considered a breach of faith toward God. He is the invisible third party Who is present everywhere where people have dealings with each other even if there are no other witnesses present. He is the guarantee for honesty in social intercourse and business . . . [The Torah goes on to describe the required oath and the 20 percent fine to be paid. The oath, administered by the court, is known as *sh'vuat pikadon*, literally, "the oath of the deposit."] This case of *sh'vuat pikadon* is a point-blank, God-derisive enrichment of oneself at the expense of one's fellow. . . it is a conscious and intentional enrichment . . . by prohibited means. It is not the sin for swearing falsely but a sin of enriching oneself by means of a false oath. . . . All these five cases [the offerings for guilt, and so on] have this in common, that they show the necessity of impressing upon ourselves . . . the danger of thinking that we have some claim to something which is really holy property [in our case the possessions of our neighbors also become holy property at the moment we Jews received our mission from God at Sinai]" (S. R. Hirsch on Leviticus 5:20–24).

"There is nothing which He is not able to do to provide for our needs, whether great or small. So one's business should be conducted in faith and honesty. One should be extremely careful not to swear by the Name of Heaven in vain [praising his goods, promising quality and price, and any of the usual advertising tactics]. The words of our Sages should be remembered (*Nedarim* 7b): When His Name is taken in vain, death appears [actually the text reads 'Poverty appears,' but poverty is like death]. So one should always avoid swearing by His Name" (Tur, *Orach Chaim*, sec. 156).

Not only are there punishment and oaths for stealing, denying obligations, and withholding other people's property, but the prohibition against doing any of these is clearly spelled out: "You [written in its Hebrew plural form] shall not steal, neither deny [your obligations], neither lie one to another, and you shall not swear by My Name to a lie; this will profane the Name of your God, I am God" (Leviticus 19:11–12). "And this injunction applies in every place, at all times, and to men and women alike. One who transgresses this injunction and denies financial obligation to his fellowman is like one who disobeys the commandment of a king" (*Sefer HaChinukh, mitzvah* 225).

"The singular form used in the Ten Commandments for these sins refers to individual lying, stealing, swearing falsely. . . . One is [however] still a long way from being a *kodosh*, holy, by simply not being an outright thief or not committing perjury. . . . [The use of the plural form in our verses] refers to such unlawfulness, such dishonesty, such swearing, which have become so interwoven into the ordinary daily business and social life of the people . . . that being universally used [they] lose the stigma of something to be avoided and can even rise to be considered as a praiseworthy and enviable act—yet before God, remain equally reprehensible as actual theft, real lies, real perjury. *Khachash* is to deny a justified accusation. It . . . affects our sincerity equally in business as in social intercourse. Neither in one nor in the other may the consideration of our own interests be the deciding factor for our words. . . . . Denial [being public] is the robber of truth, and falsehood [in secret] its thief" (S. R. Hirsch on Leviticus 19:11–12).

Many practices of denial and falsehood are common, everyday occurrences in our business dealings. In order to make a sale or to settle a transaction we perjure ourselves as to the quality, price, and quantity of the goods or services sold or rendered. Documents are signed and statements made that are false: claims from insurers, health services, or suppliers regarding defective goods returned.

"We are required to teach the people that they are required to refrain from recklessly [making false claims or promises] and to teach them that these are really vows and oaths [even in those cases where legally they do not need release. The *Raivad* comments that even when not using the Name of God, oaths and promises are still just that]" (*Mishneh Torah, Hilkhot Shvu'ot*, chap. 12, *halakhah* 2).

"During a drought a man deposited a golden dinar with a widow who placed it in a flour jar. Later, forgetting about it, she baked a cake with the flour and the coin and gave it to a poor man. When the owner returned to claim the dinar, she swore that she had never had any benefit from it. The oath was taken on the lives of her children, one of whom died shortly thereafter. When the sages heard of this, they exclaimed, 'If this is the punishment of one who takes an oath in innocence, how much more serious is the taking of a false oath?' 'What benefit did she really have,' they queried? 'She benefited from having to use less flour because of that displaced by the coin'" (*Talmud Bavli, Gittin* 35a).

"The verses include denial, theft, and false oaths to teach us that when one steals, then one denies it, then one swears falsely" (*Sifra Kedoshim*).

"One who holds his fellowman's property either as a deposit or as a loan or stolen goods or a lost article which he does not return . . . if it is demanded of him and he denies possession, he transgresses a negative *mitzvah* as it is written, 'You shall not deny.' If the perpetrator then denies under oath any of these, this is a further transgression. 'You shall not lie one to another.'" (*Mishneh Torah, Hilkhot Sh'vuot*, chap. 1, *halakhah* 8).

The Smag enumerates *lo tekhachesh* together with the positive *mitzvah* of "You shall separate yourself from a falsehood" (Smag, *Mitzvot Asei, mitzvah* 107).

"Just as the employer is forbidden to steal or to withhold the wages, so too the poor person [i.e., the worker] is warned against stealing from the employer. [He is forbidden] to dawdle a little bit here, another period later on, until the whole day is spent fraudulently. Rather he is required to guard himself regarding the time [he is paid for. Doing private work, conducting private telephone calls, or simple gossip are all examples of such fraud]. After all, the Sages freed the worker from reciting the fourth blessing of the grace after meals [after they had already taught that he should combine the first and second blessings into one, in order that he should not waste the time of the employer]. Furthermore, he [the employee] is obligated to work with all his strength (and ability). The patriarch Jacob said [to Rachel and Leah]: 'I have labored for your father with all my ability' (Gen. 31:7). For this he was blessed even in this world as it is written, 'And the man's wealth increased very much'" (*Mishneh Torah, Hilkhot Sekhirut*, chap. 13, *halakhah* 7).

"Once there was a man who studied Torah only on *Shabbat*, because all the days of the week he was busy in business. He asked a Sage: 'What is worth everything else put together and will get a person to the World to Come?' He said to him: 'You who are involved in business, be good with the world. Be careful that your fellow's money does not come into your hands, but if anything the opposite. Also, that your business dealings with everyone should be conducted with a friendly expression, and they should be in good trust. Do not be strict on other people, and do not take anything on faith lest you have to make someone take an oath. Similarly, do not receive anything on trust. Do not let anyone else's money end up in your hands so that you profit from it, even if he agreed to leave it with you, because he probably expected it back when you were able to repay, and whatever you profit from it he would have profited from it, and the result is that all the profit that you get from it is theft. If you are careful with all these things—may my lot be with yours!'" (*Sefer Ya'atzu Chasidim*, p. 194, s.v. *Ma'aseh).*

"A bailee who is entrusted with a deposit becomes obligated [*shomer chinam*] even without payment. [*Shomer chinam*] is not liable in case the article is stolen . . . unless he himself took it [in which case he becomes liable], and the courts will enforce an oath that he was not negligent but took all diligent care" (*Mishneh Torah, Hilkhot Sheilah V'pikadon*, chap. 4, *halakhah* 1).

If this is the case for a *shomer chinam*, how much more serious are the obligations of a paid bailee or one who hires another's property (*shomer sakhir*). An employee is usually considered a paid bailee, thus being liable for neglect as well as for theft and robbery. Usually agents, consultants, brokers, and salaried directors operate in effect as hired bailees. They are responsible for fraud, neglect, and not carrying out the instructions of the owners-shareholders.

"If a person loaned money to his fellow in order to buy fruit for him but the agent bought utensils, that is forbidden because he misled [literally, 'stole the consciousness of'] the lender [on purpose]" (*Tosefta Megillah* 1b).

LIFNEI IVER

Of particular importance (in connection with its view of falsehood) is the application of the Torah's injunction against putting "stumbling blocks in the path of the blind—*lifnei iver*." This term refers to the manifold activities where hidden agendas such as conflicts of interest exist. *Lifnei iver* does not always bring human retribution but "You shall fear your God" always accompanies that which is hidden in our hearts.

"And before a blind man, you shall not place a stumbling block" (Leviticus 19:14) *Lifnei Iver*.

"It is forbidden to buy stolen goods from a thief [companies or individuals who avoid paying their taxes or duties on goods are classified as having stolen *manat hamelekh*—'the portion of the king'" (*Shulchan Arukh, HaRav Baal HaTanya, Hilkhot Geneivah*; *Shulchan Arukh, Choshen Mishpat*, sec. 369, subsec. 6, *Mishneh Torah, Hilkhot Gezeilah ve'Aveidah*, chap. 5, *halakhah* 11)]. This is a grievous sin, since it strengthens the hands of those who transgress and causes them to steal again, because if they did not find a buyer they would not steal" (*Choshen Mishpat*, sec. 356:1).

"Whenever the seller asks that the goods be hidden it is forbidden" (*Mishnah, Bava Kamma*, chap. 9, *mishnah* 10).

"One is not permitted to sell to gentiles bears, lions, and anything [weapons] which can cause damage to the public [since Noachides are enjoined against murder]. Everything which is forbidden to sell to a non-Jew is similarly forbidden to sell to a Jewish robber, because by doing so one strengthens the hands of the evildoer and leads him astray. [Also applicable to anything that causes harm, physical or moral, to the buyer himself, such as cigarettes, pornography, or drugs, because we are obligated to prevent damage to another]. So too anyone who misleads somebody who is so . . . blinded by his lust and desire that he is unwilling to see the true path, all of these transgress a negative commandment as it is written, '*Lifnei Iver*'"(*Mishneh Torah, Hilkhot Rotze'ach u'Shmirat HaNefesh* , chap. 12, *halakhah* 14).

An alternative view of the *lifnei iver* concept clearly applies to direct *khazav*. This refers to the injunction against providing misleading advice: "Do not offer another advice that is detrimental to him. Do not tell him to leave a town early in the morning, knowing full well that there is a danger of him being attacked by robbers. . . . Do not tell him 'Sell your field and buy a donkey,' when you intend to buy a field and sell a donkey" (*Torah Cohanim Vayikra* 19:14).

Underlying the simple examples provided by the *Midrash* and the commentators on this aspect of *lifnei iver* is an important primary injunction relevant to our sophisticated economy: the full disclosure of all material considerations about advice given by the financial and advisory services of banks, and by accountants, lawyers, and financial analysts. This aspect of *lifnei iver* is probably more important today than ever before in human history, because of the veritable explosion in the information industries. Full disclosure of conflicts of interest, of the benefits accruing to the consultant, and of profits to be made from the ignorance of the other party seems mandatory if we wish to protect ourselves from being stumbling blocks.

Postscript

"And Chanoch walked with God" (Genesis 5:22–24). The *Midrash* tells us that Chanoch was a cobbler. Said Rabbi Yisrael Salanter, 'Is this the kind of occupation for one whom God took alive into Heaven? What mystical thoughts, what insights into the Godhead, and what spiritual inspirations he must have had while he was working! I tell you that the purpose of the *Midrash* is to teach us that Chanoch's whole being was concentrated on making sure that each stitch was true, that there was no fraud in the leather, and that the price was just'" (*Iturei Torah, Bereishit* 50).

14

בְּמַשָּׂא וּבְמַתָּן

B'masa U'v'matan—In Commerce and in Business

Greed, the *yetzer hara* for material goods, is such a powerful lust that its sanctification transforms the marketplace into a religious expression of God's holiness. Being dishonest in business means breaking faith with man and God. The major reason for dishonesty in business is uncertainty: the fear that we will never have enough to protect ourselves against the economic, physical, and political uncertainties of the future. Faith in God as the ultimate provider and source of our wealth is our real protection and provides certainty of His providence. This same faith, however, demands moral, ethical, and business accountability before the source of that wealth.

"The character trait of *emunah* ['faithfulness'] comes from the Truth, which is God. Therefore anyone who wants to draw near to God has to behave with the character trait of faithfulness in his business dealings. This is what the verse means when it says, 'A dweller in the land, a neighbor of faithfulness': when you dwell in the land and make contact with people in business, make contact with faithfulness, and do not covet anything of theirs. This matter of faithfulness is rationally obvious. When a person thinks rationally, he should realize that what is his should suffice for him and he has no right to what is not his. We have already heard that there are countries nowadays that do not have Torah at all, and through rational perception they have great faithfulness in their business dealings with everyone; people come and leave their merchandise in a particular place, go away, and come back the next day to find the money for their merchandise. If they think the price is right they take the money; and if not they take their goods and leave the money. And most of them do this out of good faith, not out of fear of the authorities . . ." (Rabbenu Bachaya, *Kad HaKemach, "Emunah"*).

Correct behavior in business is not solely or even primarily refraining from fraud, theft, or other dishonesty. Many additional requirements devolve on Jewish businessmen. They refer to competition, to everyday buying and selling, and to that partner in all transactions, the tax authorities.

"Eliyahu said: 'Once a man came and sat before me who knew the Bible but not the *Mishnah*. He said to me, "Rabbi! It happened to me once that I sold four *kors* of dates to an idolater, and I measured it out to him in halves in a dark house. The non-Jew said to me: 'You and God in Heaven know whether the amount you are measuring out to me is correct,' and I sold him short by three *seahs* of dates. After that, I took the money and I spent it on a flask of oil which I put in the place where I had sold the non-Jew the dates. The flask cracked and the oil spilled." I said to him: "My son! Blessed is God, that before Him there is no favoritism. The verse says: 'Thou shalt not defraud thy neighbor nor rob him' (Leviticus 19:13)—your neighbor is like your brother. Now you have learned that theft from a non-Jew is theft"'" (*Yalkut Shimoni* 96:7).

Limited Liability Corporation

The joint stock corporation, in which legal separation exists between the private assets of the shareholders and the liabilities of the corporation, is a major avenue for rationalizing sins in commerce and business. The limited liability aspect of the corporation seems to be viable halakhically; the rationalization however is not.

"A corporation is like any other partnership except that there exists a *tnai be'mamon*, a monetary restriction which the partners are legitimately allowed to enact. Each partner [shareholder] agrees that his liabilities will be limited to the share of capital he invests. . . . So the creditors [and anyone else] can only have recourse to the equity of the corporation [the sum of the investment of all the shareholders]" (*Mishneh Halakhot* , pt. 4, sec. 113).

No halakhic basis exists, however, for the corporate veil that frees the shareholders from the moral or spiritual obligations the Torah places on the individual Jew. The selling of *chametz* on *Pesach* (*Elef LeShlomo*, sec. 238), the observance of *Shabbat* (*Iggrot Moshe, Orach Chaim*, pt. 1, sec. 62, subsec. 3), and the injunctions against interest (*Minchat Chinukh*, pt. 3, sec. 1, pt. 4, secs. 16 and 18) have all been seen by authorities as devolving on corporations with Jewish shareholders, as well as on individuals. Thus the use of the corporate form to perpetrate fraud has been forbidden, as in this decision by the London *bet din*: "Corporation A hired an accountant to provide services which he did. . . . Then all the assets of the corporation were transferred to Corporation B [with the same shareholders], so that when the accounting fees were claimed, Corporation A had no assets from which to pay. . . . The court rules that the assets of Corporation B must be used to pay the accountant since the corporate shell was being used simply to defraud."

These halakhic decisions indicate that beyond the question of limited liability, all the moral, ethical, and spiritual obligations placed by Torah on individuals apply even when business is done in a corporate form.

Competition, Prices, Profits

"*Ona'ah*—an overcharge or an underpayment of one-sixth [of the market price or of total costs]—must be refunded, whereas an overcharge or an underpayment of more than one-sixth constitutes grounds for cancellation of the sale. [It is the waiving of rights that sets the benchmark of one-sixth, since it is assumed that people do not insist on absolute price levels.] But the overcharge need not be refunded [or the sale canceled] if the buyer waited longer than it takes to show the merchandise to a merchant or a relative before demanding the refund [or cancellation of the sale]. [Similar laws also protect the buyer from exploitation but particulars may differ]" (*Shulchan Arukh, Choshen Mishpat*, sec. 227, subsecs. 7 and 8).

"In these four periods [*Shemini Atzeret*, the eve of the first day of Passover, the eve of Shavuot, and the eve of Rosh Hashanah] butchers can be forced to slaughter their cattle, even if they have only one buyer who wishes to buy one *dinar* from an ox which is worth a thousand *dinarim*" (*Mishnah Chullin*, chap. 54). Here the talmudic Sages changed a halakhic rule, allowing the buyer to acquire part of the ox merely by paying his *dinar*, even though movable goods require, in addition to money, also an act of possession. In effect, the Sages were preventing speculation by ensuring a supply of meat for the festivals and minimizing price rises. This ruling can be compared to many protests against marketing methods that exploit temporary shortage or the pressure of special religious occasions and needs.

"Hoarders of produce, those who lend money at interest, users of false weights, and price gougers are those to whom the prophet Amos refers when he says, 'The Lord has sworn by the strength of Jacob that he will not forget their actions'" (*Talmud Bavli, Bava Basra* 90b).

"A person should not tell his fellow that he wants to buy a large quantity of wine from him, so that he sells it to him cheap, and then subsequently he buys only a little and tells his fellow that he does not want any more. Even though he can claim 'But I did not receive the goods or pay for them, rather, when you would have given me the wine I would have given you the money!' By the Law of Heaven he is obligated, because the other person can claim: 'Because I relied on your words that you would buy in bulk, I gave you a low price!'" (*Sefer Ya'atzu Chasidim*, p. 246, s.v. *lo*).

"According to the letter of the law, we do not prevent a resident of the same town from establishing a shop or profession, even next door to the shop or profession of his fellow, even though by doing so he reduces the income of the other. . . . If the entrant into the business tries to attract customers, for example by distributing gifts to children or through price competition, his competitors cannot stop him unless he cuts prices below a level sustainable for the business. . . . It makes no sense that if there is one shop or professional in a town, that it should be forbidden for someone to open another of the same type, especially in a large town where the market is large enough to provide more than sufficient livelihood for a number of shops and services. This is particularly true in a town center to which customers come from surrounding areas. And it holds to an even greater degree where the population of a town is growing and the original store captures all newcomers to the town or the street. According to all opinions, in these cases there is not even an issue of refraining from competition out of piety. [Were we to rule otherwise we would be acting immorally both in regard to the citizens who would have ultimately to pay monopoly profits and to the new entrants who wish to earn a livelihood]." (*Pitchei Choshen, Hilkhot Geneivah Ve'ona'ah*, chap. 9).

"Rav Acha the son of Rabbi Chanina interpreted [the verse in Ezekiel 18:6] as follows 'nor defiled his neighbor's wife'—that he did not infringe on his neighbor's livelihood" (*Talmud Bavli, Sanhedrin* 81a).

Another example of competition for scarce basic commodities, which was always frowned upon for ethical reasons, concerns housing. For much of Jewish history, Jews were tenants, at the mercy of unscrupulous landlords who exploited the excess demand. Already in the days of Rabbenu Gershom Me'Or HaGolah (pre-Crusade Europe), a *cherem* was enacted against those Jews who bid for occupied houses. This served as a basis during the following centuries for many communal enactments.

"This means that for three years after a Jew has been evicted from his house, no Jew may offer to rent the house [thus preventing competition leading to evictions and to increased rentals]" (*Pinkas of the Community of Padua*, 1580).

"We repeat the *herem* of Rabbenu Gershom that was adopted in our community previously: Concerning the rich who maintain several houses and plenty of living space . . . joining houses to houses so the number of houses declines and the poor cannot find places to live . . . the *parnasim* [communal workers] have to prevent this. They also have to supervise and see that the tenancy is fixed and the rentals should not be allowed to increase too rapidly" (*Pinkas Ponznan Takkanot*, 282, 283, 296).

Dina DeMalkhuta

"Shmuel said, 'The law of the land is the law'; all the laws of taxes, levies, and regulations which the king institutes in the kingdom become law [halakhically]" (*Talmud Bavli, Bava Basra* 54b, commentary of Rashbam).

This concept that the law of the land is *din*—halakhic law—simply means that all those involved in the marketplace may operate on the assumption that the same rules are being observed by all the other players. If there is a state law against insider trading or regulations providing for full disclosure of prices, quality, and financial charges, then such regulations become halakhically mandatory. One who does not fulfill them in his business operations is, in addition to everything else, transgressing Torah law.

Even where there is no non-halakhic legislation flowing from the surrounding society, the same assumed adherence to known and accepted rules of business behavior exists within the halakhic system. "The local custom—*minhag ha'makom*—or *minhag hasocharim*—the custom of the traders—has long been an established factor in the halakhic market regulations" (*Shulchan Arukh, Choshen Mishpat*, sec. 229, subsec. 2). Here, too, one is not halakhically allowed to act contrary to the accepted norms without full disclosure and agreement.

Taking advantage of other parties' adherence to the law of the land or of the custom while not adhering to them ourselves is *geneivat daat* or *nezek*—"damages." For example, infringing on patents and copyrights and copying software or tapes without permission, which may not be theft as defined halakhically, would nevertheless be forbidden because of the law of the land or the custom of the merchants.

"It seems that even in republican states with democratically elected governments, the principle of *dina demalkhuta dina* applies in regard to taxes, levies, import duties, and so on. . . . This is in accordance with the ruling of the *Rashba* (*Teshuvat HaRashba*, pt. 1, sec. 737). . . . Every government's law is *din* and is the same as that of the decisions of the king. . . . Rava said (*Talmud Bavli, Bava Kamma* 113b). The law of the king is law since he sends his agents and they cut down palm trees in order to make a bridge and we use them [which would be forbidden if the king was regarded as a robber] . . . and this applies to all the regulations of the officials appointed to implement the law" (*Yachveh De'ah*, pt. 5, sec. 63).

A major area of economic sin is that of tax evasion so that the previous ruling and the following ones are of great moral importance and must be considered when confessing.

"One who evades the taxes [and import duties] which the king has levied [the taxes could not be arbitrary or discriminatory and had to be fixed] robs the portion of the king, irrespective of whether he is a Jewish king or a gentile ruler because the law of the king is law" (*Mishneh Torah, Hilkhot Gezeilah VeAveidah*, chap. 5, *halakhot* 11–13; also *Shulchan Arukh, Choshen Mishpat*, sec. 369, subsec. 6–10). "It is forbidden to evade the levies and taxes of the king" (Maimonides, *Commentary on the Mishnah, Nedarim*, chap. 3, *mishnah* 6. See also Meiri).

As governments are impersonal, vague, and distant, it seems easier to rationalize business dishonesty in the form of tax evasion than when confronted with real people who are competitors, customers, employees, or employers. Therefore the moral results of tax evasion need to be kept in the forefront of business decisions. To evade taxes and often even to legally minimize the tax burden, false reporting or at the least a lack of full disclosure almost always exist. Such behavior involves financial sleight of hand, false declarations, varying degrees of lying, and other forms of fraud. The moral effect on the individuals is powerful and must also eventually pervade their decisions and behavior in all spheres of life. It is almost impossible to be immoral in one sphere and moral in others, so that tax immorality leads ultimately to a blurring of right and wrong.

Furthermore, in democratic countries, tax evasion in effect steals from other taxpayers and causes them to shoulder a greater-than-deserved tax burden. Just as important, however, the evader uses cost-free the physical infrastructure (roads, bridges, public transport,), the welfare system (health, old age pensions, education), and the security forces (police, army). All these are paid for primarily from taxes, and the evader uses other people's money without their knowledge and without their consent—halakhically a clear definition of theft.

Preempting in Negotiating

Masah u'matan literally means "negotiating," which is the essence of all transactions in the marketplace. Buyer and seller, like employer and employee, negotiate price, quantities, and quality of the goods or services. It is unethical for a person to preempt somebody involved in negotiating a transaction. The halakhic authorities disagree only as to whether legal action can be taken to force the interloper to return what he acquired unfairly.

"A man appointed another as an agent to enter into a marriage agreement for him. The agent went and intentionally married the woman himself. The marriage is a valid one. However, it is forbidden for one to do this [it is a fraudulent act (*Talmud Bavli, Kiddushin* 58b)]. Everyone who supplants another in this way and otherwise in commerce and business is called 'evil'" (*Mishneh Torah, Hilkhot Ishut*, chap. 9, *halakhah* 17).

"A poor man was examining a cake [for negotiating to buy it]; another who comes and takes [purchases] it is termed a wicked person" (*Talmud Bavli, Kiddushin* 58b). "If a person is negotiating to buy or hire either movable or immovable property and another preempts him and buys [or hires it], the latter is an evil person. This applies also in the case of a worker seeking employment" (*Shulchan Arukh, Choshen Mishpat*, sec. 237, subsec. 1).

"This announcement of his evil is made in the synagogue" (*Meirat Einayim, Choshen Mishpat*, sec. 237, subsec. 1). This is part of the communal pressure recognized in Judaism as an essential part of the moral environment in which we are supposed to operate.

Rav Gidel was negotiating to buy a field when Rabbi Abba came and bought it. Rav Gidel went and complained against him to Rabbi Zeira. Rabbi Zeira went and complained against him to Rabbi Yitzchak Nafcha. He said to him: "Wait until he comes to us for the festival." When he came, Rabbi Yitzchak found him and said: "If a poor man is examining a cake and another comes and takes it from him, what is the law?"

He said to him: "He is called a wicked person."

"Then why did my lord act the way he did?"

He said to him: "I did not know that Rav Gidel was negotiating for it."

"Then my lord should return it to him now."

He said to him: "I shall not sell it to him, because it is the first land that I have owned, and it's a bad omen. If he wants it, I'll give it to him as a present."

Rav Gidel didn't take it, as it is said, "But he that hates gifts shall live" (Proverbs 15:27). Rav Abba did not take it because Rav Gidel had been in midprocess of buying it. So neither one took it, and it became called "the rabbis' land" [ownerless for the students to use]. (*Talmud Bavli, Kiddushin* 59a)

"It seems plausible that the seller too has some obligation in regard to preemption of another's negotiating. This would be to tell the intruder that someone else is in the process of negotiating or already involved in the transaction. There is also the problem of aiding someone [the new buyer to commit a transgression, *lifnei iver*]. If a price has already been agreed upon, there is the problem of lack of faith on the part of the interloper" (*Pitchei Choshen, Hilkhot Geneivah VeOnaah*, chap. 9).

POSTSCRIPT

"A young *chasid* who was accustomed to devote much time to the study of the Talmud and the tenets of Chasidism, became so involved in his business that he was compelled to forgo his studies. On a holiday visit to Menachem Mendel of Kotsk, he bitterly complained of this.

"The Kotsker Rebbe answered: 'I will explain to you the passage which is recited at the end of each chapter of *Pirkei Avot*: "Rabbi Chanina ben Akashya said: 'The Holy One wanted to ennoble Israel, so he gave them numerous commandments.' But we could ask: 'What is the benefit of being duty bound to perform numerous commandments? This is a great hardship. Would not it have been better to receive only a limited number of precepts that we could fulfill correctly?' The answer is: 'The great variety of commandments makes it possible for a Jew in every occupation to obey some of God's commandments. The farmer, the planter, the house builder, and others—each one has his particular commandments to fulfill, and, thereby, to find favor in God's eyes.'

"The businessman also, by keeping away from misrepresentation, overcharging, and other commercial deception, pleases the Creator. He sanctifies himself thereby with what belongs to him, rather than with what belongs to God" (*Shem MiShmuel, Kedoshim*).

15

במאכל ובמשתה

B'MAACHAL U'V'MISHTEH—IN EATING AND DRINKING

Sins in eating and drinking are concerned not only with the *kashrut* of the food we eat or the liquids we drink. Sins exist even when the food and drink agree with all the halakhic requirements. Kosher food itself is not always a barrier to gluttony, which in the modern world extends far beyond eating and drinking. The free market ideal of "more is better than less" creates a search for a constantly rising standard of living, even if achieved through fraud and dishonesty. Conspicuous consumption, keeping up with the neighbors, and exaggerated consumerism betray standards of self-control and exert consistent pressure to earn more money. Before this barrage, ethical constraints must sooner or later collapse.

Only when the concept of "enough" is ingrained in us do we have a benchmark for measuring the sins of *b'maachal u'v'mishteh*. Modest lifestyles, the moral strength won by postponing expectations, and frugality are required hallmarks of Jewish social life. This concept of enough is maintained by a proper perspective of money's source and value. Self-made people never have enough, because the more they have, the greater success they can show.

B'maachal u'v'mishteh is inversely linked to acknowledging the source of wealth and therefore its proper use.

Jewish farmers were required to bring to the Temple *bikkurim*, the first fruits of the year's bounty from the species with which the Land of Israel is blessed by God—wheat, barley, fig, vine, pomegranate, olive, and date. Along with the offering, the farmer was obligated to make a confession—*viduy*. This is not a declaration of his agricultural prowess, luck, or hard work, not even an offering as a bribe for the future, but a simple acknowledgment of God's providence and bounty. The confession describes how a small family (Jacob and his children) went down to Egypt, were persecuted, and finally found freedom only through the Divine intervention that brought them to the land and gave the farmer his fruit. "By bringing the fruits of my land up to You, I have demonstrated that . . . my orchards and my fields stand on the soil of God and only as a son of His Covenant are they mine . . . to express his confidence that . . . possession of the land is solely because of the fulfillment of the promise made to the Patriarchs. . . . The will of God and His Almighty Power alone arranged it and no other factor participated in any way" (S. R. Hirsch on Deuteronomy 26:3–4).

When we consider the satisfaction and sense of achievement of anything *reishit*—first—then the relationship of *bikkurim* to our material wealth becomes definitive. A first job, a first home, a first business deal, a first automobile, a first acquisition are all milestones in our lives, and we must remember their source in all our *maachal u'mishteh*.

"I will tell you, Man, what is good and what the Lord demands of you: 'To do Justice, to love Truth and walk modestly before your Lord'" (Micah 6:8).

"And you shall love the Lord your God with all your heart and with all your soul and with all your might [possessions]" (Deuteronomy 6:5). "And with all your means. With all your material wealth and goods. Loving Him with all of one's possessions is to be demonstrated not only by using all of one's wealth in the service of God, but also by forgoing any gain or possession that could be earned or retained only by transgressing His law. . . . One must go so far as to sacrifice all one's possessions if keeping [or earning] them would necessitate the violation of even only one of the prohibitions [social and ritualistic] set down in the Torah" (S. R. Hirsch on Deuteronomy 6:5).

"Rabbi Eliezer says: 'Why does the verse mention with all your soul [even at the cost of your life] and also with all your possessions? To tell us that for people whose bodies matter to them more than their money, the Torah tells us to serve "with all your soul." For people whose money is more important even than their lives, the Torah tells them to serve Him "with all your possessions"'" (*Talmud Bavli*, *Berakhot* 61b).

"The *mezuzah* [that we affix to our doorposts] is connected to the things that we bring in and take out of our homes. We gather into our homes the wealth that God has bestowed upon us. All of it should therefore be in truth and in faith [as befits a house on which the Law of God is inscribed on the doorpost. This] is the secret of conducting one's business in faithfulness. In other words, what one brings into the house, that is, what one earns, should be in faithfulness. What we take out, what we spend our money on, should also be in faith. One should not spend money on useless things, or to satisfy excessive desire [fueled by advertising and the consumption patterns of our neighbors]. . . . We should suffice with necessities [or at least with modest demands] and should spend the rest of our lives in the study of Torah, on helping the poor, or acts of *chesed*, according to the blessing which the Lord bestows on us" (*Shlah*, *Shaar Ha'Otiyot*, *Mesechet Chullin*, *Derekh Chaim Tokhachot Mussar*).

"'All of your actions should be for the sake of Heaven,' (*Mishnah Avot*, chap. 2, *mishnah* 12). A person should not eat and sleep with the intention that he should be healthy and fat to engage in the matters of this world and to pursue wealth. Rather, with a full heart he should say: 'Behold, I am about to eat this so that my body should be healthy and strong to serve my Creator. Behold, I am about to go to sleep so that I will be relaxed and have a clear mind to serve my Creator. Behold, I am going to work to earn money with the help of God, so that I will be able to support myself and my family so that we will be able to serve God, give charity, act with loving-kindness and fulfill the commandments in their fullness'" (*Sefer Ya'arzu Chasidim*, p. 72, s.v. *kol*).

"Our father Yaacov, even though he was the son of Yitzchak, who was extremely wealthy—even more so than Avimelech [as the Torah states]—nonetheless the only things that he requested of God were bread to eat and clothes to wear, and nothing more. The words *to eat* and *to wear* seem to be unnecessary. But in fact they are not. Everyone knows that rich people conduct themselves in a haughty manner when they eat, scattering more food than they eat. And the same is true of clothing: they not only possess the clothes that they need, but also clothes to show off in public, of many different types of fabric. . . . Because due to our many sins, there are vanities in every age; and after enjoying them, a person falls from the high roof into the deep pit. And however happy he is now about his existence, his mourning later on about his self-destruction will be greater. So is it not better for a person to think about this at the outset, before he rushes into becoming rich, even in ways that are permitted? And even more so that a person should not work through fraud and dishonesty to increase his wealth, because then his end will certainly be as I have described. And *Hashem* will not withhold goodness from those that walk in simplicity" (Chafetz Chaim, *Sfat Tamim*, chap. 5).

"Because of our great sins, pages of Talmud are plastered on our walls, pages of *Mishnah* on our beautiful glassware and elegant tables, and all the pages of the *halakhot* of the Torah are spread over our smart clothes and the pretty dresses of our families. . . . In *Midrash Mishle*, chapter 10, it says that in the hour of judgment they ask a man about everything, about *Tanach*, *Mishnah*, *halakhot*, and other like things. When one thinks about oneself and one's life, one realizes that one lacks knowledge of almost all these books, even if one knows a little Talmud, *Mishnayot*, *Midrash*, and so on. And if a person wants to understand why and where his abilities and the time he lived went to, he will find that he exchanged his Talmud [the ability and intelligence that he was given for Talmud] for a beautiful, many-roomed home, and he exchanged his *Mishnayot* and *Halakhot* for elegant clothes for himself and his family during his life. This, then, is the explanation of what I wrote above: that the abilities given to a person to acquire our holy Torah, written and oral, are currently spread over our walls and glassware, and so forth, and that in our idiocy we have swapped a real world for an ephemeral world. The power of desire and anger expended our strength on worthless objects, and we never thought about the huge fraud of the deal. Just think: in our great sins, our actions are just like those of the African primitives who exchanged their silver and gold for toy ornaments (Chafetz Chaim, *Shem Olam*, chap. 13).

Lo Tachmod–Lo Titaveh—You Shall Not Covet and You Shall Not Desire

The urge to have possessions, clothes, and food like our neighbors is that which turns wants into needs and drives. More is always better than less.

"You shall not covet your neighbor's house; you shall not covet your neighbor's wife, his manservant, his handmaid, his ox, his donkey, or anything else that belongs to your neighbor" (Exodus 20:14).

"The social legislation [in the Ten Commandments] begins with demands upon both our actions and our words. . . . However, it is not enough to control our words and our deeds: the Torah demands that we exercise control also over our spirit and our attitudes. 'You shall not covet'" (S. R. Hirsch on Exodus 20:14).

"This precept applies in every place, in every time, and for man and woman. At the root of this precept lies the reason that this is an evil thought and causes people many misfortunes. After they firmly decide in their minds to take from the other the objects which they crave out of an evil desire, then they will take no notice of anything [and will stop at nothing]; and should the owner not wish to sell it, they will seize it by force; if the owner should stand up in defense of the property, they are even prepared to kill—as we find in the story of Naboth the Jezreelite, who was framed and murdered over his vineyard, which Ahab lusted after [to get] from him" [1 Kings 21] (*Sefer HaChinukh*, *mitzvah* 38).

"You shall not covet. You should regard the object as totally unobtainable, because it is not human nature to covet something that is completely unobtainable" (*Sforno* on Exodus 20:14).

"Many people will be puzzled by this command [not to covet]. Is there anybody who does not at some time or other covet a beautiful thing? . . . Now, let me give you a parable. A country yokel in his right senses will not hope in his heart to possess a beautiful princess, since he knows that it is impossible, just as he would not seriously hope to have wings like a bird. For this reason a thinking person will neither desire nor covet. Since he knows that the Almighty has forbidden him his neighbor's wife, coveting her would be even further from his mind than coveting the princess would be from the mind of the country yokel. He will therefore rejoice in what he has and will not turn his attention to coveting and desiring things that do not belong to him. Knowing that the Almighty does not wish to give it to him, he will realize that he cannot take it by force or through his designs" (Ibn Ezra on Exodus 20:14).

"You shall not covet. Everyone knows the question: How is it possible to lay down a prohibition which it is not in your power to keep? Even if you wanted not to covet, would not desire enter your heart in any case? The answer is that 'You shall not covet' is also a promise. A person who is careful about the previous nine of the Ten Commandments, and keeps them, will certainly not covet" (Rebbe Yechiel Michael of Zlotchov, *Itturei Torah*, pt. 3, p. 166).

"If one strongly desires that another sell him something in his possession, and he knows that the other does not wish to sell it, but that if he is pressured by words, he will be ashamed to refuse, it is forbidden to entreat him, for this would be like compelling him [which is a form of robbery, *oshek*]. And if a person of social status desires something and knows that because of the high regard in which he is held, he will not be refused, he may not ask his neighbor to sell or give it to him [even if he pays the full price] unless he knows that it will be given willingly, without any misgivings" (*Shaarei Teshuvah*, Third Gate, 43).

"And you shall not covet the wife of your neighbor; and you shall not desire your neighbor's house, his field, his manservant, his handmaid, his ox, his donkey, or anything else that belongs to your neighbor" (Deuteronomy 5:18). "If a person desires the house, wife, or utensils of his fellow, or anything similar to them which he is able to buy from him, and he considers in his heart how he can come to possess this thing, and his heart was seduced by this thing, he has transgressed a negative commandment. As it says, 'You shall not desire.' *Desire* is only in the heart. Desire leads to coveting, and coveting leads to robbery. Because if the owners do not want to sell, even when he offers them a lot of money and pesters them, he will end up stealing. As it says, 'They coveted houses and stole.' And if the owners stand up to him to save their possessions or to stop him stealing, the result will be bloodshed. You can learn this from the episode of *Achav* and

Navot. Note that you have now learned that someone who desires something transgresses one prohibition. And someone who acquires something that he desires by nagging the owners or pleading with them transgresses two prohibitions; this is why it says 'do not covet; do not desire.' And if he steals, he transgresses three prohibitions" (*Mishneh Torah*, *Hilkhot Gezeilah*, chap. 1, *halakhot* 9–12).

It is easy to translate all these injunctions against coveting into our social and business life, over and above the obvious area of patterns of consumption. An entire sector of advertising plays on our desire and lust for what other people have. Appeals to outdo others in buying designer clothes, jewelry, or motor cars, the pandering to snobbery in selling homes or offices at elegant addresses, and the barrage of advertising calling us to buy the newest fads are all the market's exploitation of our covetousness and desire. Our desires spur us to work harder and to strive for more money to satisfy them. When legal methods classified by the Rambam as transgressions fail, we turn to crime and violence.

As in all areas of business and wealth, here, too, many acts that do not seem to be criminal or even dishonest are forbidden by the Torah. The concept of *lo tachmod* includes, as already stressed, the use of perfectly legal means in order to coerce others to sell to us. This is exactly what is done when one family member bullies another to sell inherited shares or property, even when the owner does not wish to do so. On a more sophisticated level, shareholders are often badgered by unsolicited mail, by brokers, and investment bankers to sell their holdings to a takeover or raider corporation. The motivation in many cases is the coveting of the assets or success of the investment concerned.

"Two requests to an owner to sell are permitted. More than that is pestering. . . . Someone who nags somebody else to give them something as a present, transgresses *lo tachmod*. This is evident from *Rabbenu Yonah* and from the *Sefer Mitzvot Gadol* (Smag). If the owner gives the item out of embarrassment, that is close to theft. Even though it is not for themselves, asking for a friend, a relative, or a loved one is still a transgression of *lo tachmod*. The Chafetz Chaim in *Sefer Mitzvot Hakatzar* writes that a groom who pesters his father-in-law to-be before the wedding for certain gifts that were not specified as conditions is guilty of *lo tachmod*. Not just pestering for the owner to sell is *lo tachmod*, but so too is renting or borrowing" (*Teshuvat Shvet Chokhmah*, pt. 3).

Modesty in Consumption

Gluttony expressed in the constant spiral of wants translated into needs, of appeals to egoism and selfishness, and of conspicuous consumption destroys the social fabric of society. It creates jealousy, envy, and hatred, which inevitably culminate in class tensions, increased crime, and individual insecurity. Society needs therefore to provide both the parameters for acceptable standards of living and the education toward a pattern of social behavior. Judaism, both in its moral literature and in its communal norms, provides just these parameters. The individual Jew, therefore, must aspire to them if he wishes to avoid the sin of gluttony—*maachal u'mishteh*.

Role models provide a benchmark for measuring patterns of consumption within this Jewish framework. Describing the lifestyle of the *talmid chakham*—the Torah scholar, the ethical role model in Judaism—Maimonides envisages a person steeped in learning yet involved in the commerce, needs, and wants of the real world. "Such a *talmid chakham* provides for his family according to his means, yet without excessive devotion to this. His clothing should be neither that of kings [fashion trendsetters] nor that of poor men, but rather pleasant, ordinary clothing. The Torah scholar should eat his normal meals in his own house [despite the pressures and blandishments of the catering trade] and should not participate in public feasting even with scholars. It is fitting for him to eat in public [which is more expensive and conspicuous] only those meals associated with a religious precept, such as the marriage of a Torah scholar to the daughter of a scholar" (*Mishneh Torah*, *Hilkhot De'ot*, chap. 5, *halakhot* 2, 4–13).

Indeed, Maimonides was only codifying the simplicity of furniture, clothing, and lifestyle that has been an integral part of Jewish living through the centuries, an application of the spiritual demand of the prophet Micah (6:8): "You shall walk modestly before your God."

The records of the autonomous Jewish communities all mention sumptuary laws that came to limit patterns of consumption. So we find the Jewish Synod of the Rhineland rule that "no child of the Covenant shall dress after the [extravagant] fashion of the gentiles, nor wear sleeves [apparently an expression of luxury], nor shall have long hair" (13th century)."In order that we may carry ourselves in modesty and humbleness before the Lord our God . . . no one may possess cloaks of any other color than black, sleeves may not have silk linings . . . so too cloaks of sable or ermine or expensively dyed material are forbidden. . . . This does not only apply to women's clothing. Men too are restricted to the least extravagant dyes and materials" (Italy, early 15th century).

Other communities, such as Furth in 1728, prohibited the serving of tea or coffee (both in those days expensive luxury items), limited the number of musicians, and made festivities end at midnight. In Kassel, the community limited the jewelry and clothing of servants, as an indication of their masters' wealth and an incentive for conspicuous consumption. In Poznan a fine was levied for each additional guest over and above that permitted by the communal regulation.

The relationship of gluttony to the funding of the needs of the community was not lost on our ancestors. The more one spends on oneself, the less is left to fund education and social assistance to the poor, the old, and the ill. So the *Vaad Arba Aratzot*—the Council of Four Lands, the roof organization of the Jewish communities in Poland and Lithuania from the mid-sixteenth to the mid-eighteenth centuries—passed this enactment: "The leaders of the community have agreed to deal severely with the excessive and wasteful spending of money on festive meals [weddings, *brit milah*, and so on]. It is decreed that in accordance with the enactment made in 5419 [1659] in Lublin, that the number of participants at the *brit milah* be in accordance with one's financial position. One who pays two golden coins [to the community tax collector] can invite 15 people, who pays four coins invites 20 people, and who pays six coins may invite 25 people. Every ten invitees must include at least one poor person. The same principle applies with regard to weddings except that each group may add five invitees. In every case, no man shall invite more people than benefits his financial status" (Enactment 90).

The communal lenders understood that excessive spending indicates either undeclared wealth or an inability to meet communal responsibilities. In our own day, some communities have created similar restraints on the consumption patterns of their members. The *chasidim* of Gur have been limited, for example, to 300 guests at weddings, while *bar mitzvahs* are celebrated only within the family circle. Together with the *chasidim* of Belz, they are encouraged to form communities in outlying cheaper areas, in Ashdod and the Galil, for example. Along with minimal standards for housing, such restraints relieve individuals and families from having to maintain a lifestyle beyond their means, from onerous borrowing to finance such a lifestyle, and even from being involved in unethical business behavior to fund it.

Ethical exhortations and communal pressure are essential to put needs and wants into the correct perspective. At the same time a basic premise serves as the foundation. "Ben Zoma said, 'Who is rich? He who is happy with his lot, as it is said, "When you eat from the toil of your hands, happy shall you be, and it shall be well with you" (Psalm 128:2); happy is this world—and it shall go well with you in the world to come'" (*Mishnah Avot*, chap. 3, *mishnah* 1).

Referring to this same verse in Psalms, the Admor Menachem Mendel of Kotsk said, "If you eat only of the toil of your own hand, it will be well with you." "It is important in life," he said on another occasion, "to see how far you have come up the ladder and not only to see how far you still have to climb."

"For whom is it proper to praise in his wealth? To one for whom it is sufficient to use what he has and does not worry about what he does not have. He does not chase after easy profits to increase his wealth through robbery and oppression, fraud and deception. He will be blessed that he will not require charity and assistance from others [because he does not aim constantly for more than he can afford] which will save him from depression (*Talmud Bavli*, *Berakhot* 6b). He will be rewarded in the world to come because he comes clean of crime and there is no *chamas*—violence—in his hands. However, there is one who never has enough, and even when he has plenty of money he cannot say 'enough.' The only passion he has is to increase what he has. Of such a person the prophet Jeremiah said, 'Let not the rich exalt themselves with their wealth [rather] be wise and recognize [know] Me . . . because this I desire, saith the Lord' (Jeremiah 9:22)" (Maimonides, Commentary on *Mishnah Avot*).

"How do you learn to be happy with your lot in life? . . . One time-honored method is to think of those whose life situation is worse than yours. When you have all the parts of your body in working order, you are indeed wealthy. If you do not believe this, visit any hospital. . . . You will soon see how fortunate you are. As an old Arab proverb has it, 'I had no shoes and complained, until I met a man without feet.' But above all, a person can be happy with his lot in life only when he sees himself and his existence as part of some greater plan, when he knows that his task is to further these ultimate values which transcend petty human longings" (Irving M. Bunim, *Ethics from Sinai*, vol. 2, pp. 8–11).

"Go to the ant, you sluggard, and learn her ways" is understood throughout the world as laudable advice. It is an incentive to economic striving and an encouragement for the accumulation of more and more. Not so did our Sages see this verse in Proverbs (6:6). They saw the ant's life as the epitome of foolishness and wasted endeavor. "After all," they said, "the ant eats only two grains of wheat and lives for but one season, yet it labors ceaselessly to amass a fortune" (*Talmud Bavli*, *Sotah* 48b).

Postscript

"The sin of this generation [the builders of the Tower of Babel] is similar to that of Adam, Cain, and his sons. The latter were not satisfied with the munificent bounty bestowed on them by a generous Deity and the material plenty available to them. Instead of using their status of being created in God's image for the perfection of their spiritual aspects, they devoted themselves to the perfection of crafts, husbandry, and agriculture . . . to improve the natural order of things which the Deity in His wisdom provided as sufficient for the needs of mankind . . . greed and aggression . . . rules of private property. . . . What is mine is mine and what is yours is yours" (Abarbanel, *Bereshit* 3:4–11).

"And they [the tribes of Gad and Reuven] came to Moses and said, "We will build sheep pens for our livestock and cities for our children.' This shows that their primary love was their possessions [their flocks] since they placed these first. They should have thought first of their children whose spiritual future they were endangering by removing them from the midst of the tribes of Israel and from the sanctity of the Lord of Israel [by asking for the attractive pastures of Transjordan]. Just as they grasped first at enhancing their wealth so they were exiled first and lost all their possessions" (*Midrash Rabbah*, *Bamidbar* 32:16).

16

בְּנֶשֶׁךְ וּבְמַרְבִּית

B'neshech U'v'marbit—By Interest and Usury

Charging interest for lending money is not intrinsically immoral. Logic tells us that charging interest for lending money makes no less sense than charging rent for a house or a fee for hiring a car. However, Torah commands with regard to money that as an act of charity you forgo the interest due on a loan made to a fellow Jew. One is obligated to do acts of charity to all people, but this particular form of charity is only mandatory when it relates to coreligionists; it could not be viable as a one-way street in a world that does not return the kindness. Such acts enable recipients to break out of the poverty cycle or to avoid the dangers of temporary illiquidity. We are also obligated to avoid oppressing the debtor through any act. At the same time, we are enjoined against wasting the money lent to us or postponing repayments, or avoiding settlement of our debt. Hiding behind the limited-liability provisions of the corporation in order to protect our assets may be legal, but maintaining our standard of living at the expense of creditors after bankruptcy is surely immoral.

"If [when] you lend money to My people, to the poor man who is with you, you shall not behave toward him like a creditor; you shall not impose interest on him. If you, in any way whatsoever, take your neighbor's garment as a pledge, return it to him by sunset, for this alone is his covering; it is his garment for his body. On what shall he bed? Were he to cry out unto Me, I will hear, for I (God) am gracious" (Exodus 22:24).

"And if your brother becomes impoverished and his hand wavers beside you, then you shall support him, even the stranger who has become only a sojourner, so that he may live with you. But you must not take any interest or increase from him, and you must fear your God, and your brother's life shall be bound up with you. You must not give him your money at interest and you must not give him your food for increase. I, God, am your God, Who brought you out from the land of Mirzrayim to give you the land of Canaan, to be God to you" (Leviticus 25:36).

"You must not pay your brother any interest, be it interest in money or interest in food: no interest at all, nothing that could be construed in any way as interest. You may pay interest to the stranger [but] to your brother you must not pay interest, so that God, your God, may bless you in everything to which you may put your hand in the land to which you are coming, to take possession of it" (Deuteronomy 23:20).

"'But you must not take any interest or increase from him, and you must fear your God.' Man's thoughts are greatly attracted by the idea of taking interest, and it is difficult to him to keep aloof from it. He tries to persuade himself that it is permissible, since his money would otherwise remain unemployed. For this reason the Torah had to state 'And you must fear your God'" (Rashi on Leviticus 25:36).

"The juxtaposition of the phrase 'and your brother's life shall be bound up with you' with the sentence 'But you must not take any interest or increase from him' alludes to the fact that any person who lends on interest is not really alive." (Baal HaTurim on Leviticus 25:36).

"You must not take interest from anyone who is your brother, even if the borrower gains from the transaction. Why? Because the main reason for the prohibition on taking interest is that it removes the character trait of trust from a person. The eyes of every businessman are raised to God, since he does not know whether or not he will make a profit. But the person who lends money on interest knows in advance and fixes from the outset the profit he will receive. He has confidence in his possession of the lender's pledge, and his heart is turned from God. And the reason why the borrower also transgresses is because he causes the lender to sin by removing the sense of trust from him. You can see this by observing those who lend on interest: most of them have a paucity of faith, and are hard-hearted and far from charity, since they have no trust in God" (Kli Yakar on Leviticus 25:36).

"We have already discussed in detail the concept on which the prohibition against taking interest from a fellow Jew is based. We have shown there that Jewish Law definitely does not regard charging interest on loans per se as illegal or morally wrong. If it did, it would not also have prohibited, with equal emphasis, the paying of interest by the borrower, and the prohibition against charging interest would not have been restricted to loan transactions among Jews. Rather, not charging—or paying—interest in loan transactions among Jews is a splendid act of homage to God, expressing our recognition of Him as the Master and Owner also of our movable possessions even as the release of the land and the institution of the Jubilee Year demonstrate our acknowledgment of His dominion and control over our landed property. . . .

"Judaism teaches us that our money is not our own; it is ours only under certain conditions. The One Who is truly entitled to exercise control over our money is God. It is He Who commands us to place some of the assets, which are His but which happen to be in our hands, into the hands of our brother, to enable him not merely to obtain the necessities of life, but also to help him maintain and continue his business activities. God's behest is that, in return for the obligation the borrower has assumed to reimburse us with an equal amount of money for a given time, the money, which until then was our money, becomes the borrower's at the moment it passes from our hands into his.

"Thus, the money with which the borrower does business is not ours at all, but his own. His earnings from it will be a product of his own work with his own money, and will therefore be entirely his own. If we were to demand any part of these earnings from him, we would be taking *neshech*, a 'bite,' as it were, from his personal assets. At the same time, it would represent *tarbit*, 'an increase' in our assets. It would not be a compensation for earnings we could have made with the principal, for we had no right to withold the loan from the borrower in order to use the money for our own business, seeing that it is God, the true Owner of all things, Who has placed the money at the disposal of another. Therefore, even if the borrower has made earnings with the principal or if the lender could have made earnings with it, any interest charged or paid on the loan would be *neshech* and *tarbit*.

Here we have the great impact of the Jewish concept of *tzedakah*, which is indisputably part of *tzedek*, that which is just and right: what in the eyes of the giver would seem to be an act of lovingkindness is, in the eyes of God, no more than the repayment of a legal debt . . ." (S. R. Hirsch on Leviticus 25:36).

"Rabbi Dimi taught, 'If anybody has a financial claim (rent, debts, and so on) on another person and knows that the debtor is not able to pay it, the creditor must go out of the way of that person in order to avoid arousing the feeling of shame in his mind. After all, the Torah demanded "You shall not behave toward him as a creditor, it will be as though he had killed him twice—drowned him and burnt him even as it is written 'You have delivered us into the power of man; into fire and water we are come' (Psalm 116:12)''" (*Talmud Bavli, Bava Metziah* 75b).

"Whoever fulfills the injunction not to lend his money on interest accepts upon himself the yoke of the Kingdom of Heaven, and whoever rejects this injunction removes from himself the yoke of Heaven" (*Yalkut Shimoni, Parshat Behar*, Leviticus 25:36).

"The full knowledge of when money is lent at interest is something that often only the lender knows so the verse admonished 'And you shall fear your God' (Leviticus 25:36) since all things done in the secret recesses of the heart require this fear" (*Talmud Bavli, Kiddushin* 32b).

The connection between interest and the Exodus from Egypt referred to in Leviticus 25:36 seems strange at first glance. Yet the biblical reference is strengthened by the realization that the prime message of the Exodus is God's mastery over both the forces of nature and the affairs of men. This Lordship is expressed inter alia in Divine Providence that provides all our needs. A person who lends money at interest demonstrates thereby that he cannot rely on God's bounty. The interest charged is a sign of refusal to do for others the acts of mercy that God does for him. So the Sages taught that who lends his money at interest denies the Exodus from Egypt: "One who lends money at interest denies the God of Israel and the Exodus from Egypt and will not be resurrected from death at the End of Days. In this world his material possessions will diminish and eventually be destroyed" (*Shulchan Arukh, Baal HaTanya, Hilkhot Ribit ve Hilkhot Iska*, chap. 1, *halakhah* 2.

Question addressed to Rashi: Upon the dissolution of a partnership it was found that part of the assets consisted of unsecured loans granted to non-Jews. The major partners wished to leave the collection of his share of these unsecured debts to the junior partner (knowing full well that it would be far more difficult for him to do so than for them). Failing this, they were prepared to collect his share, provided they were compensated for their efforts.

Answer: To leave the collection of the debt from the non-Jews to the junior partner and in case he fails, to leave the debt unclaimed (thus causing him a great loss) is a wicked act, not fitting for a holy people adhering to the tenets of the Torah. We are commanded "Thou shalt restore it to him and thou mayest not hide thyself" (Deuteronomy 22:2). The major partner cannot claim "let me die with the Philistines" and allow his money to be lost as well, since he was a party to the loan and is under obligation to collect it. Neither is he entitled to any compensation for this collection, other than the customary commission. (*Responsa of Rashi*, ed. I. Elfenbein [New York, 1945], no. 80)

Issur Ribit—The Injunction against Taking Interest

"There are ten *mitzvot* concerning loans. Two positive *mitzvot* to lend money to the poor of Israel and to return the object or goods left as collateral whenever the debtor requires it. The eight negative *mitzvot* are: not to oppress the debtor, not to obtain collateral through coercion, not to delay returning the collateral to the poor owner whenever needed, not to demand collateral from a widow [poor or rich], not to accept as collateral things required for the satisfaction of essential foodstuffs—*chaye nefesh* but literally, the maintenance of the very soul, the creditor may not lend his money at interest, the borrower may not borrow money at interest [thereby waiving the protection given by the Torah], nobody is permitted to be involved in the transaction even as a witness, a scribe, or as a guarantor" (*Mishneh Torah*, *Hilkhot Malveh UeLoveh*, introduction).

"What is *Neshekh* [forbidden by the Torah in Leviticus 25:26–27] and what is *Tarbit* [also forbidden]? One who lends four dinarim (in order to later receive) five [25-percent interest]. This is *Neshekh*. *Tarbit* is one who earns through investment [literally, *Peirot*]" (*Mishnah*, *Bava Metziah*, chap. 5, *mishnah* 1). *Neshekh* is paid to the creditor for the *hamtanat ma'ot*, the time during which he has no use of the money.

"Biblical interest [*neshekh*, according to the previous *mishnah*] is earned through a straight loan, clearly delineated, involving *hamtanat ma'ot* with repayments [of principal and additional interest.] Such interest may be reclaimed through the courts who will force and physically punish the creditor until his soul departs [or until he repays the interest. This even when the debtor originally agreed, since he does not have the power to forgo that which the Torah insisted on]" (*Shulchan Arukh*, *Yoreh De'ah*, *Hilkhot Ribit*, sec. 161, subsec. 5).

"The person who lends at interest transgresses six prohibitions [this includes a stumbling block in the path of the blind—the debtor who is not allowed to pay interest]. The borrower transgresses two prohibitions, including a stumbling block [in this case before the creditor who is forbidden to lend at interest]. The witnesses and the scribe and the guarantors each transgress one transgression—you shall not place upon him interest [since they enable the creditor to effect the loan. However, there is also *lifnei iver* in these cases where the transaction could not have taken place without them]. Any agent or one who works for a finder's fee to bring borrower and lender together transgresses *lifnei ever*" (*Mishneh Torah Hilkhot Malveh UeLoveh,* chap. 4, *halakhah* 2).

"We should have no involvement with a loan made between a borrower and a lender at interest. In other words, we should not provide them with any surety or guarantee, not act as witnesses for them, not write a document specifying the interest to be paid. For it is stated, 'Nor shall you set interest upon him,' and the Talmud (*Bava Metziah*) explains that this prohibition is aimed at those who are indirectly involved in this loan, such as the guarantor, witnesses, and scribe. Furthermore, it explains that the lender is also included under this prohibition, in addition to all the other injunctions that apply specifically to him. In total, as Abbaye is quoted there as saying, the lender violates six precepts; the borrower, two; and the person who is otherwise involved with them, one. The root of the precept is that the good, benevolent God desires the settled, communal existence of His people that He chose. This is the reason why He commanded us to remove this source of trouble from their path, so that one should not swallow up the life-force of another without the other's realizing it, to the point where he finds his house empty and bereft of every good. Because this is how interest works. Everybody knows it, and that's why it is called *neshekh*. But now, since the guarantor, witnesses, and scribe will all distance themselves from this thing, people generally will refrain from it" (*Sefer HaChinukh*, *mitzvah* 68).

"If he earns an income through buying and selling (on credit or as a result of price changes or as a silent partner in an investment) this is *avak ribit* (*Tarbit*) and forbidden by rabbinic law, [as distinct from Torah, forbidden interest earned simply for the loss of the alternative use of money as a result of waiting to be paid]. If one earned such money [the courts cannot be used to claim repayment], one should nevertheless return it in order to be clean before Heaven" (*Shulchan Arukh*, *Baal HaTanya*, *Hilchot Ribit ve Hilkhot Iska*, chap. 1, *halakhah* 4).

"Even when the interest is less than a *shaveh prutah* (only of insignificant value) it is forbidden. It is true that this sum cannot be claimed in a court [just as in the case of theft which is forbidden but then a *shaveh prutah* cannot be claimed]" (*Shulchan Arukh*, *Yoreh De'ah*, sec. 161, subsec. 1).

The Rama, quoting the Tur, writes there that interest of *shaveh prutah* is forbidden irrespective of whether it is earned on a loan (forbidden—*Mi de oraita*) or earned through commerce (forbidden by rabbinic decree).

Interest earned through commerce, rabbinic interest, payments for goods bought on credit, installment payments, mortgage loans, and even payment paid to compensate for inflation or change in the exchange rates—all of these require a *heter iska*. Contrary to common assumption, the *heter iska* is not an amulet nor is it a legal fiction that enables one to evade the Torah's injunction against interest. In order to be halakhically valid, the agreement needs to fulfill certain requirements. It is essential that it refer to a real *iska*, commercial transaction, undertaken with a viable assumption that a profit will accrue. This projected profit needs to be at least twice as great as the 'interest.' Mortgages that closely resemble loans rather than investments create special problems. Some authorities (*Vayechi Yosef, Dinei Ribit*) hold that these have all the halakhic characteristics of a loan as distinct from an investment and so cannot be included in a *heter iska*. Others, bearing in mind the characteristics of the mortgage—fixed period, the lien on the property, payments clearly specified in the contract, and so on—maintain that mortgages require a specially designed *heter iska* (*Iggrot Moshe, Yoreh De'ah*, pt. 2, sec. 62).

Subterfuges, such as placing Jewish money with a non-Jew, who then lends it to another Jew, ostensibly as his own, are considered *ribit me deoraita* and so, strictly forbidden.

It makes no difference whether the money is lent to a poor man or a rich man.

Not only is monetary interest forbidden, so too are any benefits, material or otherwise, the lender may receive.

"So, if the borrower [as appreciation] gives the creditor more than the amount of the loan, even if there is no demand for him to do so, and even if the debtor does not state that the additional amount is interest, this is forbidden. If the debtor at the time of repayment says, 'I give it to you as a gift,' it is forbidden irrespective of whether the interest was paid before the loan was received [in order to persuade the creditor to lend the money] or after the loan was repaid—this is *avak ribit*. The creditor must be careful not to benefit from the debtor . . . in any action which the latter was not accustomed to do . . . definitely not a public act like living in the debtor's apartment. It is forbidden to lend money at interest even to one's children or family. One may not do work for somebody on the understanding that he will later do the same for you . . . except where the work is identical in all respects" (*Yoreh De'ah*, sec. 160).

"Rabbi Shimon Bar Yochai says, 'How do we know that someone who borrows from his friend [interest free] and was not in the habit of greeting him *Shalom* is forbidden to greet him like that after receiving the loan? Because the Torah says, "Nothing that could be constituted in any way as interest"—even speech —is forbidden [This includes blessing the lender]'" (*Talmud Bavli*, *Bava Metziah* 75b).

Because of fluctuations in prices or in exchange rates, it is forbidden to borrow goods on the understanding that one will return them at a later date; the price increase is regarded as interest.

There exists an obligation to make interest-free loans (*Gemilut Chesed*). One cannot refrain from charging interest and assume that one is fulfilling one's Jewish obligations. On the contrary, one *is obligated* to make interest-free loans. This is not simply an act of benevolence but a halakhically binding obligation.

"It is a positive commandment to lend to the poor of Israel, and it is a greater *mitzvah* than charity. . . . A poor relative comes before other poor people, and the poor of one's own town come before the poor of another town. . . . It is even a *mitzvah* to lend to a rich person who needs a loan in his hour of need [temporary illiquidity, which could possibily lead to bankruptcy], and to be kind to him even with words by giving him appropriate advice" (*Shulchan Arukh*, *Choshen Mishpat,* sec. 97).

". . . By making this loan he performs two *mitzvot*: he sustains the poor person, and he also saves the poor person the humiliation of having to beg for money . . ." (*Prisha*, *Choshen Mishpat,* sec. 97).

"'If you lend money to My people, to the poor man who is with you.' The verse seems to repeat itself. It should have said simply, 'If you lend money to the poor man. . . .' But the Torah first calls this person 'My people,' then 'the poor man,' and then 'your neighbor,' when it says, "If you, in any way whatsoever, take your neighbor's garment as a pledge." The reason for this is that since the Torah wished to command us about two separate things, it used two introductions, as if to say that you are obligated to lend to a poor person from two perspectives. The first is from the perspective that he is part of the nation. It is the practice of kings that when their people and servants lack food, anybody can lend to them, relying on the king to repay the debt. This is because it is the king's obligation to feed his people, and a person who gives to them thus in some sense actually gives to the king himself. Therefore he can be sure that the debt will be repaid. Similarly, a poor man is part of 'My people.' He places his needs on *Hashem*, and the person who helps him thus lends to *Hashem*. Because really the person who lends to the poor lends to *Hashem*, and not to the poor person. The second perspective is that the poor man does more for you than you do for him. As the Talmud concludes, '[I]f *Hashem* loves poor people then why does He not feed them?' To save us from Gehenom [because He forces us to behave charitably and to share our wealth]. The lender gives the poor man temporary sustenance, but the creditor receives an eternal world as his reward. The creditor gives a penny, and *Hashem* rewards him amply" (Kli Yakar on *Shemot* 22:24).

"The root of this commandment to lend to the poor is that God wanted His creations to be used to acting with loving-kindness and pity, since it is a praiseworthy character trait. By the preparation of their bodies with good character traits they will thus be fit to receive goodness. As I have already mentioned: good descends to the world because of good, not its opposite. When God does good to those that do good, His desire to do good to the world is fulfilled. And were it not for this reason, He would provide the poor with everything they need. But out of His kindness, may He be blessed, we were made His agent for our benefit. For these reasons our Sages warned us against not fulfilling this commandment. One who has money and does not lend it interest-free is despicable, outlandish, perverted, and abominable until he is comparable to those who worship idols. How pleasant, admirable, merciful, and blessed with a multitude of blessings are those who fulfill this *mitzvah*" (*Sefer HaChinukh*, *mitzvah* 66).

"When God first conferred upon the slaves in Egypt the right to own property by virtue of their status as human beings, He cemented these individuals into a community not by force of sheer personal need but by the bond of duty that binds them together as members of one society. . . . It is not the less-affluent man who should have to turn to his more prosperous brother for help; no, it is the duty of the more fortunate individual to seek out a neighbor who could benefit from his abundance. The rich need the poor much more, and in a much higher sense, than the poor need the rich. All that the poor man can get from the rich is assistance for his material needs. But for the rich man, the poor are in fact the means that enable him to carry out his sublime spiritual and moral task of paying to God the tribute He expects in return for every penny He has bestowed upon us. By enabling us to become property owners, God has reserved for Himself the right to enlist our property in His service. The prime beneficiary in this arrangement is to be "His people," the society to be created through the spirit of His Law. This is the spirit of *tzedakah*, the Jewish concept of righteousness as a matter of duty, which to this day is responsible for the miraculous survival of the Jews as a nation and which finds its most potent expression in our obligation to lend money to those in need of it. This is also the spirit to which any claim to interest must yield" (S. R. Hirsch on Exodus 22:24).

"A person has to conduct himself in this [the *mitzvah* of lending money to people in need] just as with the *mitzvah* of charity. That is, he has to give the money with a warm expression, not with an angry scowl. As it says in *Avot de Rabbi Natan*, chapter 13: 'Receive everyone with warm expression. How so? This teaches you that even if a person gives his friend all the presents in the world, if his face is scowling at the ground when he does so, the Torah sees him as though he had not given anything.' And this is how the *halakhah* is fixed [in *Yoreh De'ah* 249:3], and it is also the case with lending someone money: you have to be careful not to look at someone disparagingly, heaven forbid! Rather, give someone a loan with a warm, friendly expression. He should imagine to himself: If I had to obtain some favor from my friend, how much would I want my friend to relate to me warmly. So too he should relate to his friend. And this is how Rashi explains the verse in *parshat Mishpatim*: 'If you lend money. . . .' This is what he says: 'Another explanation. "The poor man"—that you should not treat him disparagingly when you lend to him because he is My people. "The poor man with you"—see yourself as though you are poor.' And this is particularly true if the borrower is crushed and low, and with the loan that you are making to him you are strengthening him so that he will be able to support himself so that he will not return to dependence on other people" (*Chafetz Chaim*, *Ahavat Chesed*, chap. 23).

"It is a positive commandment to lend to the poor of Israel, as the Torah says: 'If you lend money.' You might have thought that this means that lending is optional; that's why the Torah says: 'Lend, lend to him.' And this commandment is greater than giving charity to a poor beggar, since the beggar is in a state where he is forced to beg, whereas this person has still not reached that state. And the Torah is strict on a person who refrains from lending to a poor person, as it says, 'Be careful lest your eye would look in an evil matter upon your brother, the needy man.' Everyone who presses a poor person for repayment and knows that he does not have anything transgresses a negative commandment. It is forbidden for a person to show himself before his debtor at a time when he knows that he has nothing, even to walk in view of him, and even without demanding repayment, so that he does not traumatize him or embarrass him. And just as it is forbidden for the lender to claim his debt, so too it is forbidden for the borrower to conceal his friend's money in his possession, to tell him to go away and return another time. This is when he has the money, as the Torah says: 'Do not say to your neighbor, "Go away and return another time."' The person who lends on interest also transgresses the prohibition 'You shall not behave toward him like a creditor'" (*Mishneh Torah, Hilchot Malveh u'Loveh*, chap. 1, *halakhot* 3–4).

"The highest form of charity . . . is one who supports the hand of an Israelite who becomes lowly [poor] and gives him a gift or [an interest-free] loan or creates a partnership with him [the partnership being even higher since the poor has not shame from it]. . . . In order that he should not descend to the level that he needs to beg, even as it is written and 'you will strengthen him, the stranger and the convert, and he shall live with you' (Leviticus 25:35), that is, you will strengthen him until he will be steady and not fall so that he requires assistance" (*Mishneh Torah*, *Hilkhot Matnat Aniyim*, chap. 10, *halakhah* 7).

"The Commandment is not to claim a debt from a poor person when he has no money to pay. For the root of this *mitzvah* is that we should aquire for ourselves the character traits of loving-kindness, pity, and mercy. Once they are rooted in us, we will be fit to receive goodness. Then the desire of *Hashem* will be fulfilled in us, because *Hashem* wants to do good in this world and in the world to come" (*Sefer HaChinukh, mitzvah* 67).

Postscript

Maimonides includes the laws of interest where they rationally belong, in the laws of borrower and lender. However, the *Tur* and *Shulchan Arukh* include the laws of interest in *Yoreh De'ah*, that portion of the Codes that deals with things that are ritually forbidden and those that are ritually permitted, following the laws of idolatry. These include the laws of kosher food and those of *Niddah* (a woman's purification after menstruation); although interest is a monetary issue, nevertheless the prohibition follows from the law of things that are ritually forbidden.

Menachem Mendel of Kotsk said, "This is because the interest is *treif*, not pure, just like unkosher food."

17

"And You Shall Do That Which Is Right and Good in the Eyes of God"

The list of sins in the marketplace continues, almost endless in its challenges and yet always solvable with the guidance of Torah and *mitzvot*. Nothing in the *Al Chet* recited by Jews does not impinge directly or indirectly on money; there is no immorality Judaism's teachings cannot help to overcome or at least to mitigate.

***B'azut Metzach*—By Brazen Arrogance**

The arrogance of those who consider themselves more important than others and the only people with a right to the world's wealth and benefits leads to economic sin. Such people browbeat their competitors, employees, and debtors to squeeze the last drops of economic benefit from them. They default on debts, oblivious to the suffering of their creditors, and put themselves above the laws of man and God by ignoring the rules and regulations of economic agencies. Their arrogance allows them to ignore the pain and loss they cause to others. The rabbis made much of the fact that *damim*, literally, "blood," also means "money."

"And you shall not bring an abomination [idolatry] into your house" (Deuteronomy 7:26). [In Proverbs 16] it is written, "The arrogant heart is an abomination before the Lord." Said Rabbi Yochanan in the name of Rabbi Shimon bar Yochai, "Every person who has arrogance, it is as though they worship idols" (*Talmud Bavli*, *Sotah* 4b).

"Lest you eat and are satiated and your herds and flocks multiply themselves, and your silver and gold increase . . . and your heart becomes haughty, and you forget God" (Deuteronomy 8:12). Said Rabbi Nachman bar Yitzchak, "This is a warning against arrogance, since it is also written previously [in verse 11], be extremely careful that you do not forget God, and do not keep His commandments, His social laws, and His statutes" (*Talmud Bavli*, *Sotah* 5a).

Bitzdiat Reah—Ensnaring People

Naive clients can easily be misled by high powered salesmen into borrowing money that they cannot ever repay or into buying goods and services they neither need nor can afford. Misrepresenting business information can fool shareholders or creditors into making decisions that are to their detriment. Moreover, takeovers and buyouts are often accompanied by strategems close to plotting and conniving.

Betzarut Ayin—By egoism and selfishness

Bitzomet Yad—By breach of trust

B'lashon Harah—By gossip and slander

The Way Out of the Maze

"And do that which is right and good in the eyes of God; therefore it will go well with you, and you will come and take possession of the good Land that God has sworn to your fathers, to thrust away all your enemies before you as God has spoken" (Deuteronomy 6:18,19).

"Our conduct is to be guided by the standard of 'that which in God's judgment is upright and good.' Our Sages interpret this as a principle that extends even further than the demands of God's Law with regard to our social behavior, as follows: we are not to obey merely the dictates of right and duty explicitly set forth in the Law, but we must also let ourselves be guided by that spirit of goodness and right which is implicit in these stipulations. The principle includes, first and foremost, the concept of fairness that commands us not to avail ourselves of a right—even if we are legally entitled to it—if the advantage we would gain from claiming that right is disproportionately small compared to the advantage the other party would gain if we were to waive our claim. . . . When there is a higher, positive, and good purpose, you should be ready to forgo even those rights to which the law entitles you . . ." (S. R. Hirsch on Deuteronomy 6:18–19).

"Our Sages had a beautiful homiletical interpretation of this. They said that this [refers to] compromise, and going beyond the letter of the law. What they meant by this was that the Torah has earlier said that you should keep His precepts and testimonies which He has commanded you; and now it tells you that even where you have not been explicitly commanded, apply your intelligence and do that which is straight and good in the eyes of God, because he loves straightness and goodness. This is a major issue, because it would be impossible for the Torah to specify a person's every interaction with his neighbors and friends, all his business dealings, and his activity on a local and national level. So after it mentions a lot of them such as 'do not be a talebearer,' 'do not take revenge' and 'don't bear a grudge,' it proceeds to lay down a general principle: do that which is straight and good in everything, to the point where you will include compromise and going beyond the letter or the law" (*Rambam*).

"Some landowners' fields bordered the banks of a river. Rav ruled that the bottom one has the right to use the water first, while Shmuel ruled that the top one has the right to use the water first. They did not dispute the case where the river flows; they argued only when the landowners dam it and use the water for irrigation.

Rav Huna bar Tachlifa said that since there is no explicit ruling in favor of Rav or Shmuel, the *halakhah* is that whichever landowner is stronger wins.

Rav Shimi bar Ashi came to Abbaya and said to him: Would my lord teach me regularly?

Abbaya said to him: I need my own time to learn.—Would my lord teach me at night?

He said to him: I have to irrigate my field with water.

He said to him: If I irrigate my lord's field during the day, would my lord teach me at night?

He said to him: Very well.

Rav Shimi bar Ashi went to the owners of the upper fields and said to them: the owners of the lower fields have the right to use the water for irrigation first. He went to the owners of the lower fields and said to them: the owners of the fields have the right to use the water for irrigation first. In the meantime, he dammed the river and irrigated [Abbaya's field, which was in the middle].

When he came to Abbaya, he [Abbaya] said to him: you have acted like both [Rav and Shmuel].

And he did not eat the fruit [of the field] that year" (*Talmud Gittin* 60b).

Tosafot on that:

"You have acted like both." He [Rav Shimi bar Ashi] thought that since it was ruled that whoever is strongest wins, he was able to act cunningly. . . . "And he did not eat": to let it be known that he [Rav Shimi bar Ashi] had not acted on his [Abbaya's] instructions. And perhaps he sold the fruit, because this was not a case of theft but [the issue was one of] acting according to the paths of peace.

"The truth is that the desire for money blinds people, so that they permit themselves to do forbidden things. But they [the Sages] said about this issue that a person is recognizable by his pocket; that his intelligence should overcome his desires; and he should become completely reconciled with himself, even if that means that he possibly has to live like a pauper, so that he should not be a wicked person before God. And also that it is clearly true that those who search for God will not lack anything, and the person who lives in straightness lives in security.

"When a person goes to business one should say, 'For the unification of the Holy One and His Divine Presence I am going to this work, and I have faith that God will give me every blessing in this business, and that this work should be the medium for God to give me every blessing in everything I do.' And when God provides a profit, then one should remember God, because He is the one who has given you the strength to succeed." And when God showers down blessings then one will not become arrogant. On the contrary, one will be humbled and embarrassed: "What am I that He has brought me so far?" One will be extremely scared that The Holy One is paying the reward in this world, or that He is testing us to see how we will use the money . . ." (*Shaar haOtiyot, Mesechet Chullin,* chap. *Ner Mitzvah*).

"Although we see that most people are not manifest thieves in the sense of openly confiscating their neighbor's belongings and depositing them among their own possessions, most of them get a taste of theft in the course of their business dealings by allowing themselves to gain through their neighbor's loss, saying 'Business is different.' However, many prohibitions were stated in regard to theft: Do not steal, Do not rob, Do not oppress, and You shall not deny, and A man should not speak falsely against his neighbor. A man should not deceive his brother. Do not push back your neighbor's boundary. These varied laws of theft take in many of the most common types of transactions in relation to which there are many prohibitions. For it is not the overt, acknowledged deed of oppression or theft alone which is forbidden; but anything which would lead to such a deed and bring it about is included in the prohibition. Concerning this our Sages of blessed memory said (*Sanhedrin* 81a), 'And he did not pollute his neighbor's wife' (Ezekiel 18:15); he did not infringe upon his neighbor's occupation" (*Mesillat Yesharim*, chap. 9).

"Another point about the character trait of conceding [one's rights] in cases involving other people. The Rambam wrote at the end of chapter 10 of *Hilkhot De'ot*, and I quote: 'His business dealings should be in truth and faithfulness. . . .' It holds a fortiori that a person should not get into arguments that are not his. As our Sages of blessed memory said, 'Who has not done good?' This refers to someone who comes before a court with power of attorney. And do not initiate legal procedings even if you are justified in doing so, because it is shameful for a Torah scholar to cheapen himself before judges, because our Sages of blessed memory said of both litigants in a court case that 'You [the judges] should regard both of them as wicked,' and they [judges] do not distinguish between people. Therefore it is a poor characteristic in a person to passionately desire the implementation of the law. Even if his fellow is liable to him by law, he should concede what he can. And if he is unable to do this, then the law will bore through the mountain. But even then he should not act in haste, but rather in moderation. Then a man will cleave to the Divine characteristic of mercy. Regarding non-Jews, it is a great *mitzvah* to sanctify God's name through monetary matters, and to return [money] to them, so that they should say, 'Blessed is God, the Lord of Israel'" (*Shlah*, *Shaar haOtiyot*, *Ot vav*, "*Vatranut*").

"The Holy One Blessed Be He desires only honesty, as it is said (Psalm 34:21), 'God protects the honest ones,' (Isaiah 26:2); 'Open ye doors so that there may enter a righteous nation, a keeper of trusts,' and (Psalm 101:6), 'My eyes are to the trusted men of the earth, that they may sit with me,' and (Jeremiah 5:3), 'Are your eyes not to faithfulness?' Even Job said about himself (Job 31:7), 'Did my steps deviate from the path? Did my eyes follow my heart? Did anything adhere to my palm?' Regard the beauty of this comparison in which concealed theft is likened to a thing which sticks to a person's hand. Here, too, though a man does not actually go out and steal, it is difficult for his hands to be entirely clean of theft, for the eyes, instead of being ruled by the heart so that they do not find pleasing to them what belongs to others, pull the heart after them to seek rationalizations for the acquisition of what seems beautiful and desirable to them" (*Mesillat Yesharim*, *Pratei haNekiut*, p. 117).

"Rabbi Yehushua the son of Levi said: the *egla arufa* [the offering brought by the leaders of the community that was the closest to an unidentified corpse found in a field] existed only because of stingy people. As it says (Deuteronomy 21), 'They will answer and say, "Our hands did not spill this blood, and our eyes did not see."' Did we really imagine that the elders of the court were spillers of blood? Rather [it means this]: This person did not come into our hands, and we took leave of him without food; we did not see him and let him leave him without an escort" (*Talmud Sotah* 38b).

"If a person wants to sell a piece of land or a house, and two people come to him and want to buy it for the same price, and neither of them owns land contiguous to what he is selling [otherwise he would have the right of first refusal], then if one of them is a resident of his town and the other is not, he should sell to the resident of his town. If both of them are residents of his town but one of them is a resident of his neighborhood and the other is not, he should sell to the resident of his neighborhood. If one of them is a friend whom he regularly spends time with and the other is not, he should sell to his friend. If one of them is his friend and the other is a relative, he should sell to his friend, as it says 'A close neighbor is better than a distant brother'; but compared to anyone else his relative takes precedence, except for a Torah scholar who takes precedence even over a neighbor and a friend whom he regularly spends time with. This order of precedence is a commandment of the Sages, defining the way to fulfill the verse 'And you shall do that which is right and good in the eyes of God'" (*Shulchan Arukh haRav* (*Baal HaTanya*) *Hilkhot Mechirah*, sec. 5).

"A porter who breaks a cask of wine while moving it from one place to another on a level path [normal method of transferring the cask] is guilty of negligence and is liable to pay for the damage [he caused to the owner of the goods]. . . . Nevertheless, it is a *mitzvah* to act *lifnim mishurat hadin* and give the porter his hire, if he is poor" (*Tur*, *Choshen Mishpat*, sec. 304, subsec. 1).

This is based on the talmudic case of a person who brought his workers to Rava to adjudicate their case. They had broken his wine casks, and he had seized their cloaks as damages. When Rava ordered the employer to return the cloaks, he was asked, "Is this the law"? "Yes" replied Rava, "and you shall walk in righteous ways." Then the workers asked for their wages. The owner was distraught when Rava ordered him to do just that. "They broke my property, they are not required to pay for the damages, and now I have to pay their wages. Is this the law?" "Yes," replied Rava. "They are poor, and you are obligated to walk in righteous ways."

"Reuven has been operating a liquor store for many years. Now Shimon, who is wealthy, has other businesses, and no dependents, wishes to open a similar firm. Asked if Shimon could be prevented, I answer that by law, Shimon cannot be prevented. However, according to the Bach (*Responsa,* sec. 12) the court can force Shimon to waive his legal rights and refrain from opening the proposed store—*lifnim mishurat hadin*—since this is an act of Sodom. Even were this not so, the court should at least use verbal pressure not to open the competing store" (*Teshuvot, Tzemach Tzedek, Choshen Mishpat*, sec. 418, subsec. 11).

"Why is the book of Deuteronomy called *Sefer Ha Yashar* [the Book of Righteousness]? Because it is written there, 'And you will do that which is good and righteous in the eyes of the Lord'" (*Talmud Bavli, Avodah Zarah*, 25a).

"If the land is held as security for the creditor, he is not required by law to return it but he is required by the ruling 'And you shall do that which is good and righteous (*Talmud Bavli, Bava Metziah* 16b).'"

"Rabbi Yehudah said in the name of Rav, 'One who had land sited between two brothers or between two partners [shares in a nonquoted corporation?] and thereby causes them trouble or loss, is cheeky [and one should not do this], but they cannot force him out.' 'Rabbi Nachman said, "They can force him out [to sell] since a person does not have the right to cause financial harm to others. However, they cannot do so under the claim of *bar metzrah* [the right of first refusal given by *halakhah* to the owner of adjacent property (or shares?) to buy it at market prices].' The Sages of Nehardea said [and this is the *halakhah*], they can force him to sell under the law of *bar metzrah* because it is written, 'And you shall do that which is good and righteous in the eyes of God' [and a person should not do anything which is not moral or righteous even if he has a legal right to do so]" (*Talmud Bavli, Bava Metziah* 108a).

"And you shall love your neighbor as yourself" (Leviticus 17:18). Rabbi Akiva said, "This is a major principle in Torah." "This is because many *mitzvot* in the Torah are included in this one. One who loves his neighbor as himself will not steal his money, will not commit adultery with his wife, will not oppress him financially, will not encroach on his livelihood, and will not harm him in any way" (*Sefer HaChinukh, mitzvah* 243).

"Ben Azzai taught, 'These are the generations of man,' is a greater *mitzvah* as it is written, 'For the Lord made man in His Image' (*Sifra*). Even if one does not insist on one's own honor, one should still be meticulous regarding the honor of another [so that when one oppresses or defrauds or harms others, he is in effect acting against Him, in whose image man was created]" (*Sefer Mitzvot Katan Yitzchak of Courville*).

"You shall not reap the edges of your field [*Peah*]. . . . You shall leave them for the poor and the stranger [like all gifts to the poor, *Peah* is not withheld from the poor non-Jews for the sake of peace]" (*Talmud Bavli*, *Gittin* 59b).

"The Lord wished that this People, whom He chose, should be adorned with every good and precious quality, that they should have a blessed soul and a generous spirit. . . . The soul is influenced by one's activities. . . . There is no doubt that when a man leaves one part of the produce in his field and makes it ownerless [the same applies spiritually to all of the forms of wealth] so that those in need can benefit from it, you will see in his soul a decent and generous spirit and a fulfilled spiritual satisfaction. . . . Whereupon the Eternal Lord will bless him and satisfy him with this goodness. On the other hand if someone gathers everything [that legally belongs to him] into his house [firm, business, or corporation] leaving no blessing behind him from which the poor could benefit [ignoring the fact that] having seen the field with the crops growing tall [like seeing the wealth of the rich about them] they felt a yearning and a desire for it to fill their soul when they grow hungry, he [the owner of the wealth] displays beyond any doubt an evil heart and a mean spirit. Then evil will equally befall him. "By the yardstick with which a man measures, by that he is measured" (*Talmud Bavli*, *Sotah* 86; *Sefer Ha Chinukh*, *mitzvah* 216).

"If one went ahead and nevertheless reaped everything he has to give some of the produce to the poor, the owner may not derive any pleasure by giving them [to a particular poor person, since they are ownerless]. Rather, any of the poor can take it even against the will of the owner [there is an opinion that this applies to charity money levied by the community on a person, which has not been paid to charity]" (*Sefer HaChinukh*, *mitzvah* 216).

A major factor pressuring people to insist absolutely on their rights, to disregard the needs of others, and often to engage in business immorality is the need for instant gratification or for enjoying everything possible. Yet the Torah commanded us not to eat of the fruit of our trees before the fourth year (Leviticus 19:23). This is *orlah*, and only trees like men have an *orlah*—men are born uncircumcised, and trees have an uncircumcised fruit. The *orlah* of trees is removed by the fourth year and the *orlah* of men by the removal of their foreskin. Of the entire creation, only the trees disobeyed God—by not producing fruit which would taste like themselves as he commanded. Adam also disobeyed by stealing of the Tree of Knowledge. Nachmanides (Ramban) explained that this law of *orlah* in fruit comes to honor God by our not eating of the first of our produce until we are able to harvest the entire fruit of one season. In the first three years the yield is unfit to honor God because it is sparse; there is no taste or good smell, and many trees do not produce any fruit at all before the fourth year. Therefore, we postpone our enjoyment of the fruit till after we have first honored the source of all our wealth, God.

"Anyone who steals money worth the equivalent of a *prutah* or more transgresses a negative prohibition, as it says, 'Thou shalt not steal'. . . . It is the same whether he steals the money of a Jew, the money of a non-Jew who worships idols, or whether he steals from an adult or a minor."

Maggid Mishneh on that: "The law about [stealing from] the non-Jew comes from '*hagozel u'ma'achil*'(*Sanhedrin* 113b) [where it says that] robbing a non-Jew is forbidden, and the same goes for stealing from him; and the same appears in other places" (*Mishneh Torah*, *Hilkhot Geneivah*, chap. 1, *halakhah* 1).

"It is forbidden for a person to conduct himself with words of flattery and undue compliments, and he should not say one thing and think another. Rather, his outer self should be as his inner self. And it is forbidden to mislead [literally, 'steal the opinion of'] people, even a non-Jew . . . even one word of flattery and of deception is forbidden . . ." (*Mishneh Torah*, *Hilkhot De'ot*, chap. 2, *halakhah* 6).

"Now, illegal retention [of another's property], robbery, and theft are [essentially] one matter. The purpose of all three [injunctions] is that no man should take the possessions of another in any way whatever, since in these three ways people despoil one another. Nevertheless, Torah gave them all in detail and warned us against each one by itself. Rava said: illegal retention and robbery are one and the same; then why did we divide them [into two precepts]?—to make every such an act the violation of two negative precepts. The meaning of this theme and its main import to my mind is that the more that God wished to remove us, for our own good, a great distance [from something], the more He increased for us the number of injunctions about it. In addition the Omnipresent God wished to make the Israelites meritorious, and He therefore gave them a great many *mitzvot* and added on for them a great many prohibitions where it would be possible to give them the same instruction in one expression of warning—such as here. It was possible to adjure us in a general way, "Do not take anything of value from other people unjustly." Yet the injunctions about the matter were increased for us, so that we can receive increased reward for abstaining from the transgression, and these injunctions [against fraud, oppression, theft, robbery, cheating] are incumbent on men and women, in every place and at every time" (*Sefer HaChinukh*, *mitzvah* 228).

"This is the rule: All movable goods acquire each other. How so? [If] he [the buyer] drew produce (literally, "fruit") from him [the seller] but did not give him money, he cannot retract. [If] he gave him money but did not draw produce from him, he can retract. But they said: He who punished the men of the generation of the flood and the generation of the Tower of Babel, He will punish him who does not stand by his word" (*Mishnah Bava Metziah*, chap. 4, *mishnah* 1).

The Rishonim ask: It is clear that in all these cases [mentioned by the Braita: the men of the flood, Babel, and so on], the people concerned were guilty of serious crimes against their fellowmen, but why are these four cases appropriate to the case discussed here in the *Mishnah* and the *Gemara* of one who retracts from a contract? The Rosh and Meiri explain two of these cases. Pharaoh was singled out because he regularly broke his promises [throughout the events narrated in chapters 8, 9, and 10 of Exodus]. The Rosh points out that the generation of the flood were known for their deceit. Meiri adds that the Jerusalem Talmud explains that the generation of the flood used to take advantage of legal loopholes to steal in such ways that they could not be penalized in court. Thus, these instances were singled out to deter a buyer or seller who is contemplating doing the same.

As to the other two examples, it is interesting to note that the people of Sodom are said by the Sages to have had no pity on their fellowmen, and to have insisted on taking even the smallest amount to which they had a legal claim (*Avot* 5:13). Concerning the generation of Babel, a *midrash* (*Pirkei deRabbi Eliezer*) says that God destroyed the Tower of Babel because He saw that its builders cared more about a fallen brick than about a fallen person. Thus the people of Sodom and the builders of the Tower may have been singled out in order to deter a buyer or seller who is concerned only with his legal prerogatives and not with his fellowmen, and is thus prepared to cause another person distress in order to make a profit (Steinsaltz Notes, *Talmud Bavli*, *Bava Metziah*, 48a).

"Movable goods are acquired by the buyer drawing them into his possession. Indeed, by doing so he finalizes the transaction even if he has not yet paid any money, and neither party can retract. However, if the buyer has not yet drawn the merchandise into his possession, either party may retract, although the person who retracts at this point is subject of the imprecation of 'He who punished'" (*Shulchan Aruch*, *Choshen Mishpat*, 198:1 and 204:1).

"Rabban Shimon Ben Gamliel said that by virtue of three things the world endures. Truth, justice, and peace, as it is said, and you shall administer truth and the justice of peace in your gates" (*Mishnah Avot*, chap. 1, *mishnah* 19).

"Moreover, he [Hillel] saw a skull floating on the surface of the water and he said to it, 'They drowned you because you drowned others, and those who drowned you will themselves be drowned'" (*Mishnah Avot*, chap. 2, *mishnah* 7).

"Rabbi Yochanan said to them [his disciples], 'Go and see which is the good way which a person should follow faithfully.' Rabbi Elizer said, 'A good eye! [an attitude of kindness and goodwill toward other people's concerns and possessions].' . . . Rabbi Elazar ben Arakh said, 'A good heart [receptive only to the good so that one is not capable of deserving evil]'" (*Mishnah Avot*, chap. 2, *mishnah* 14).

Rabbi Meir of Premislan once refused a bribe, but the person found a way to put it in the pocket of the Rabbi's coat without his knowing about it. All day long the Rabbi found he was unable to judge cases clearly and could not arrive at any decisions in cases before the court. He dismissed the court, and when he put on his coat, he put his hands in the pocket and exclaimed, "Now I know what was clouding my intelligence and my judgment."

"There is no better antidote to the weakness of the heart than a combination of the qualities of truth and justice. Neither bonds of friendship, nor mighty young cattle, nor weapons and body armor can protect one like the helmet of Truth and the shield of Justice. On the day when I shall bequeath to you the heritage vouchsafed to me by the Creator, I shall transmit to you primarily the quality of trustworthiness by virtue of which I acquired these possessions. 'For with my staff I passed over' to acquire 'the permanent bread and its drink offering' and, alas, the Lord blessed me until now. It was my faithfulness that led me into places where my kinsfolk could never have brought me and bestowed upon me an inheritance greater than that of my parents. It invested me with authority over those greater and better than myself, and I prospered and became useful to myself and others. Be therefore zealous for the welfare of others, even *lifnim mi shurat hadin*, beyond the letter of the law; keep your word and do not evade your public or private promises made either verbally or in writing, either before witnesses or in private. Reject and avoid fraudulent, underhand, and unlawful practices. . . . Do not partake of anything, large or small, that is not yours. . . . Know that one who accustoms himself to dubious things will inevitably resort to willful activity, just as one who takes a small amount in the beginning or takes something secretly will eventually take much and in public until he is known as a confirmed liar, robber, and embezzler. . . . Be proud of your moral values and content in your faithfulness, for there is no greater nobility and no more glorious inheritance" (The last will and testament of Maimonides).

"One who wishes to sensitize himself spiritually will break his evil urge—*yetzer hara* for money, and will extend his hands gracefully to others. Everything he does for the welfare of others he will do with grace and pleasure. . . . When he feeds the hungry, he will give them of the best and most pleasant food; when he clothes the naked, it will be with the finest of his garments" (*Yoreh De'ah*, sec. 248, subsec. 8).

EPILOGUE

A Psalm of David.

Lord, who may sojourn in Your Tabernacle, who shall dwell in Your Holy mountain?

[From the continuation we learn that one who desires to become close to the Almighty must first implement God's teachings with regard to Mankind, so,]

He who walks in faith [that God provides all his needs, so that his sustenance may be earned with integrity] creates Justice [through economic righteousness] and speaks the truth in his heart [revealing the faults in his goods and does not steal the mind of his neighbor]. He who has no slander on his tongue [does not deprecate the goods, services or prices of his competitors nor cast aspersion on their integrity] nor done evil to his fellow [by damaging his property, health or aesthetic enjoyment nor encroaches on his livelihood] nor cast disgrace on anybody [through harassment, browbeating or shaming employees or debtors]. In whose eyes that which is despicable [eating habits, rowdyism, reckless driving] is repulsive but honors those who fear the Lord. He has sworn and does not change his oath [in order to evade his obligations or default on his business contracts]. Who has not lent out his money at interest [even not through strategems or legal fictions while lending his money interest free to the poor] nor has he taken a bribe against innocent people [to obtain business advantages or to escape fines levied for breaches of the law or commercial regulations]. He who fulfills all these shall not falter or waver forever.

Psalm 15

Index

About the Author

Meir Tamari is director of the Centre for Business Ethics at the Jerusalem College of Technology, consultant to the Jewish Association for Business Ethics in the United Kingdom, and dean of the American Association for Jewish Business Ethics. After making *aliyah* from South Africa to a religious kibbutz in 1950, he served in the Bank of Israel in corporate research from 1960 to 1990, achieving the position of chief economist, office of the governor. Dr. Tamari is the author of numerous books and articles—academic and rabbinic—on business ethics, small firms, risk evaluation, and entrepreneurship and is publisher of the *Business Ethics Newsletter* in Jerusalem. The pioneer of a special course on Jewish ethics and economics at Bar-Ilan University, Dr. Tamari has lectured internationally and has served as consultant to various governmental bodies in the United Kingdom, France, and the United States.